JJ THE CPA HERE!

I0504272

I would like to dedicate this book to

my late grandad & mentor, Omar Abbott Slayter, CPA!

I want to share my inspiration for all I do to

my kiddos, Chloe & Cooper!

I want to thank my one and only,

Amanda, for absolutely making this possible,

and for all her love, support, encouragement and editing!

I want to express my gratitude to

all my clients that have made me JJ THE CPA

and provided the questions over 26 years that I answer in

this book!

JJ THE CPA HERE!

Wow! Thanks for buying my book! I am absolutely honored!

WHAT IS IT ALL ABOUT?

These are the most asked questions by clients over the last 26 years of my career. I have been advising clients, just like you. I think I have brought a unique perspective to my clients in that I want to be fully aware of everything my clients are involved with, when it comes not only to their taxes, but their banking, insurance and business issues. So after advising thousands and thousands of clients, individuals and businesses alike, I have compiled in this book, for you, the answers to client's most asked questions.

Why is this a great book for you? Well, I appreciate you already picking it up, and the benefit you will gain is each chapter, each subject, has the potential to save you money and time with the very issues you are dealing with day in, and day out. And, for only the cost of this book! What a bargain, when you compare to what I charge my clients to receive this same information. Now, for my wonderful clients who have picked up this book, thank you! I love you for it! So much! The difference in what I provided to my clients, is their consulting with me allowed the suggestions, recommendations and advice to be tailored to their specific situations. And with that being said, the additional benefit you will have, even if you are not a client of mine, is you will be better equipped on what to look for in your current financial picture, and better prepared to ask your own advisors on these same issues, so they can best advise you.

The thing to note with all advisors, including myself, is we can only address what we are aware of, and that is up to our clients to help us be aware of the circumstances they are in, as all clients are unique and special to their own needs. So again, this will help you discover secrets from a CPA's perspective, that will give you more information on what to ask your current advisors, so they can better serve you. One size does not fit all, but these questions are one size fits all. My answers are to share what I advise my clients of, but the premise of my answers are the foundation to get you moving in the right direction. So again, thank you for buying my book, and look for more to come! For more information about these subjects, be sure to find me on social media as I release a new video every single day on subjects I am dealing with clients on. Just search JJ the CPA on any social media platform. The value just continues.

With reading this book, you will find the additional advice I am providing on social media to compliment the foundational information you will gain in this book!

Ready? Me too! Let's rock!

DISCLAIMER: THESE ARE MY VIEWS AND OPINIONS BASED ON MY EXPERIENCES. THESE ARE NOT THE VIEWS OF ANYONE ELSE OR ANY OTHER COMPANY. I AM NOT REPRESENTING ANY COMPANY. THIS IS NOT A SOLICITATION. THIS IS NOT AN ADVERTISEMENT. THIS IS NOT A SALES PIECE. THIS IS NOT BEING PRESENTED IN CONJUNTION WITH MY SERVICES THAT I AM LICENSED IN. THIS IS NOT TO BE USED TO DETERMINE IF YOU SHOULD BUY ANY SERVICES, INSURANCE OR PRODUCTS FROM ME. ANY AND ALL INFORMATION IN THIS BOOK SHOULD BE CONSIDERED SUGGESTIONS AND NOT ADVICE. YOU MUST SEEK AND RELY ON THE ADVICE OF THE PROFESSIONAL YOU WORK WITH IN THE AREAS DISCUSSED IN THIS BOOK. YOU ARE

REALLY MISSING THE ENTIRE POINT OF THIS BOOK IF YOU TAKE ONE SUGGESTION IN MY BOOK AND ACT ALONE. THE ENTIRE PREMISE OF THIS BOOK IS TO SHARE A GENERAL IDEA TO TAKE TO YOUR ADVISOR SPECIALIZING IN THE NEED YOU HAVE. IF YOU SOLEY RELY ON ANY SUGGESTION IN THIS BOOK, TO TAKE ANY ACTION, YOU ARE ACTING ALONE AS YOU ARE NOT CONSIDERED A CLIENT OF MINE, UNLESS YOU HAVE SIGNED A WRITTEN ENGAGEMENT LETTER FROM MY OFFICE, AND HAVE PAID ME MONEY FOR SERVICES. I LOVE YOU, BUT YOU KNOW IN THE WORLD WE LIVE IN TODAY, WE HAVE TO STATE THESE TYPES OF THNGS. IF I MISSED ANYTHING IN THIS DISCLAIMER TO PROTECT MYSELF AND THE COMPANIES I WORK WITH, CONSIDER THOSE OTHER

PROVISIONS THAT ARE IN MY FAVOR WERE IMPLIED. THIS IS JUST A BOOK. THANK YOU! OKAY, HERE WE GO!

TABLE OF CONTENTS

BUSINESS TIPS, SECRETS............................136

WHO IS YOUR TEAM?

What Professionals Should I Hire to Help Me With Personal and Business Matters?

JJ THE CPA here. Every person and every business should have these 4 core professionals involved with their personal and business decision making process.

*CPA/EA who specializes in what you need.

*A banker specializing in what you need.

*An attorney who specializes in what you need.

*An insurance professional who specializes in what you need.

Why did I repeat in each line that the professional listed *needs to specialize in working with what you need?* Because you need to ask and ensure that particular professional works with what you need because... not all do. You won't just google "I need a Doctor" and then expect that Doctor to work on any and all medical services you need. Right? You would ensure the Doctor works with what you need. So, you need a professional that works with what you need. Make sense?

When you are narrowing done who you need on your team advising you, next ensure they work with what you need personally or with your type of business, so you are getting the best advice based on the professional's experience with you what you need.

You can pretty much ask 2 questions to gain the best clues if the professional works with what you need.

*What percentage of your clients are businesses like mine? Or if not needing businesses services, what percentage of your practice works with this kind of service.

*What would be the first thing you would need from me to know if we are a fit?

If someone has at least 5-10% of their practice working with what you need or your type of business, that is pretty good. And if they can answer the second question quickly and concisely or can email you a list quickly, that is a great first sign they know your issue(s) or business.

Something to note. There are really two types of businesses, which are determined on what they sale; the revenue of the business.

*Service industry (sales based primarily on labor sold).
Examples would be: Doctor, lawyer, accountant,
counselor, personal trainer, consultant, hair stylist, etc.

*Buy and selling items (sales based on product sold).
Examples would be: Clothing store, restaurant, wholesale,
Amazon, candy shop, toy store, grocery store, etc.

So, when considering which professionals to work with
related to your business, at least be sure they are working
within your industry type and with your type of business.
Example: I do not work with the second type of business,
for the most part, as I work with the service industry. So
with that being said, my practice is made up of 55% of my
services to businesses (45% to individuals) and of those
businesses, 95% are in the service industry, of which 10%
are dental practices. I would be an excellent fit to work

with Dentists. I would not be a fit to work with a company that sales equipment to Dentists. Make sense? That really could apply to all the professionals listed.

When considering which professionals to work with related to your personal needs, be sure they are already working with that particular need, with at least 20% of their practice made up of servicing that need. Example: My practice is 45% of individual services. Note, that of those individual services, 80% are to individuals who own businesses. I would be a great fit to work with business owner's individual taxes, and since 20% of my individual services are for non-business owners, I would also be a good fit for individuals who do not own businesses. But let's take that one step further. None of my practice deals with personal budgeting. So even though I provide individual services, I only provide those services related to tax planning and preparation. Make sense?

With CPAs, there are two major categories of CPA firms. Tax and audit. If you need both services for your business, get separate CPA firms, as a firm that audits your financials cannot provide advice as they must remain independent. If you don't have a business, then of course you want a CPA firm that does individual tax work. Not all CPA firms perform payroll or bookkeeping services, so you should inquire if they perform these services. For my CPA practice, we refer our clients to experts in the area of payroll and to a separate company that performs bookkeeping services because it is cheaper for the client and... those other companies are experts in... payroll and bookkeeping. I am an expert in tax planning and tax preparation. I understand payroll and bookkeeping of course, but I am specialized in income taxes.

With EAs (Enrolled Agents), they specialize in tax, as their designation and oversight comes from the IRS. An EA must pass an exam by the IRS on tax and obtain annual continuation education on tax matters, which is key. For bookkeeping and payroll services, they would be similar to a CPA firm; some do, some don't. I will always recommend a CPA first, as I am CPA, but I see no issues in someone hiring an EA for tax services, as long as they meet other criteria of being experienced in the your area of need.

With banking needs, you want to find a specific banker at a bank that meets your needs. Having a relationship with a banker (the person) will be key in obtaining banking advice related to your needs; whether business or personal. I would say most banks offer banking needs and loans to both individuals and businesses.

However, not all banks specialize in the type of loan you may need or with the type of business you are, or the industry you are in. Some banks don't provide mortgages or lines of credit. All banks have a maximum they will loan any one customer, and that is different from bank to bank. You may want to have your personal banking needs at a different bank from your business needs so the two types of loans are considered separately.

Here's an example:

Let's say your business buys and sells widgets. If the banker and bank doesn't know that type of business, it may prove more difficult to get the "amount" of loans you need as they may not understand why you need your loans; or the actual risk.

A bank not specializing in businesses that buy and sell widgets may very well provide you a loan, but not the type of you loan you need; which in this example would be a healthy line of credit. And so on.

An example for individuals: Most banks provide auto loans, however, they may not provide the most competitive rates. Why? Because they may not specialize in those auto loans.

With insurance, whether for personal or business, if you check out their website and inquire, it should be more clear and easily evident what type of insurance they provide. And if they provide that type of insurance, they should specialize in it.

However, while an insurance company that specializes in liability insurance, may not specialize in professional liability insurance, homeowner's liability, personal liability umbrellas or insurance on construction projects. Why does that matter? Because if an insurance professional doesn't specialize in it, most likely the insurance company doesn't specialize in it, which can easily lead to the insurance premiums costing more because they don't have a risk pool large enough to offer lower premiums. So most everyone is going to have several insurance professionals with several insurance companies covering and reducing their various risks.

With attorneys, they typically are like Doctors in that they are very upfront with the type of law they practice.

A heart surgeon will be very clear they don't provide any services, advice or recommendations related to your brain, teeth or feet. Typically, this will be the same with an attorney. There are several categories of attorneys, and it is rare attorneys cross-over. It is possible a law firm may provide multiple services, but I have never come across a law firm that provides all legal services. The major categories are:

*Business law

*Estate planning

*Personal injury

*Criminal law

*Family law (mostly divorce)

It wouldn't be unheard of if an attorney or law firm provided services for both one and two above. However, for the remainder, most attorneys or law firms are going to really zero in on that specific type of law. Overall, when selecting the team of professionals to work with, do not be afraid to have several types of professionals within one type of service needed. However, most likely what will be key is to NOT have several professionals that provide the same service to you, as you want the advice given to you, in whatever area it is, to be all encompassing of the issues you have in that area. Example: If you have two life insurance professionals, one may recommend a type of life insurance that includes a long-term care rider of some kind, but if you have another insurance professional who also specializes in life insurance, they may recommend a separate policy for long-term care insurance, and thus, you could be over-insured, which could mean you are paying premiums for insurance you already have; and could instead be using those premiums to buy other or more insurance of another kind.

PLANNING
PROTECTION
INSURANCE
RETIREMENT
LIFE
ASSET
DISABILITY
WHOLE
PERMANENT
LONG TERM
LEGACY
FAMILY
BUSINESS

Insurance Angles

Do You Really Need to Hire an Insurance Professional?

YES!!!!!!!!!!!!!!!!!!!!

JJ THE CPA here. Yes, hire an insurance "professional!" Don't hire a salesperson. And don't do anything without considering the advice of your insurance professional that specializes in the type of insurance you need or are considering.

In my opinion, the difference between a salesperson and a professional is how they present the sale you. Both are going to sale something, so get that in your head. Anything you buy, someone sold you.

Dental work, medical procedures, tomatoes, dinner, etc.

However, I believe a salesperson "talks you into something" you don't agree with and uses your emotions against you to buy nonetheless. A professional will still inquire of how you feel about something, but will present information to you, that you should be convinced to buy based on data that you need it. We will always include emotions, but it should feel good to you when you buy anything.

Know this, you will NOT find an insurance professional that is an expert in all types of insurance, just the same as you will not find a Doctor who specializes and knows all types of medicine.

There could be an insurance agency with multiple departments that may help you, but I don't know of any insurance agency that handles literally every kind of insurance possible.

If you find one, they will be a jack of all trades and master of none, as the saying goes. Makes no sense for you to sacrifice expertise for convenience of working with one company.

Overall, most types of insurance can fit into 1 of 3 categories, which means most insurance professionals specialize in one of these; possibly the first and third ones listed.:

*Property & casualty (related to tangible assets)

*Life, health, disability & long-term care (related to the condition of a human)

*Liability (related to protecting assets or you if something going wrong)

Don't do anything without considering the advice of an insurance professional that specializes in the type of insurance you need.

Insurance Angles

Why Do You Get Insurance?

Like Any Type of Insurance. Why?

JJ THE CPA here. Why do you get life insurance, disability income insurance, long term care, etc.? Why do you get any of these? It is called reducing the risk. Mark, my mentor said this to me, and it just changed everything. We get insurance, any kind, to protect ourselves against risk.

Risk of what? Losing your assets. Current and future. Let me ask you this. If you stop thinking about the cost of the insurance but about the risks you need to reduce, would that change everything for you as well, when it comes to determining what insurances and amounts you need?

It should, because the cost of insurance is never going to cost more than the risk it could reduce, ever!

If you purchase an expensive watch, ring, car, boat and/or house, the first thing you do is get insurance on them in case something happens. Are you expecting something to happen; a car accident, a house fire, etc.? No, of course not. It is just what we do. We insure the things that are important to us and provide a level of protection for our assets. A replacement of them, and not having to use other assets to replace assets lost. So, my question to you is, are you not the most important asset of them all?

Another aspect that I have discussed many times, is another reason you would get those insurances, is to protect the assets we have so it does not affect retirement assets.

What is the first thing that people think about when getting disability income insurance? That it will provide income if I become disabled so I can live on the income from the policy. Yes, of course and it is tax free as well, but the other reason to have that is if something were to happen to you and you became disabled, you would not have to deplete your assets, including retirement assets, to continue your way of living. Think about that. You could be in a situation where you are partially disabled for let's say, 18 months. Look around right now at your current situation; if something happened to you and you could not work for 18 months, could you and your family survive financially? I will be honest, if I did not have disability income insurance, my answer to that question would be no. If I took the receivables in my business, the cash in my savings, my retirement and I just kept my current lifestyle in place, I would be out of money quickly. The number one reason homes foreclose in America is due to disability, because many do not have enough set aside or enough disability income insurance to outlast, even a short period of time, being unable to earn income.

Whether you get disability income, long-term care, whole life, term life insurance, etc., if you are not a believer in it from the standpoint of, I will probably never use it, you are really fooling yourself. I have had clients look at me and say, I am healthy, and my parents lived for a long time, so I do not need any life insurance. Great. What about those that are left behind? Because guess what, you are not buying life insurance for yourself, you are buying it for those left behind. Think about that for a minute.

It is always better to be prepared.

If you have these insurances in play and something happens (which would never happen to you, right), then the ones that you are leaving behind are taken care of. If you are disabled, you are not depleting your retirement assets to continue your current lifestyle or putting everything at risk by having nothing left after you deplete your bank account and investments.

Insurance Angles

Do I Really Need Disability Income Insurance?
Like Seriously?

JJ THE CPA here. Let's talk more about disability. Why? Because most of you are going to think when you get disabled that you are laid up and can't do a thing, and/or it's probably from a car accident, and that insurance will cover you.

That simply is not true, as there are countless situations that can cause you to become disabled. Here is the thing you need to know over 50% of disability in America is partial disability, and of that, 50% is disabilities from mental issues (migraines, stress, depression; not mental illness, mental issues) and for less than 18 months.

There are over 40 million Americans with some type of disability.   And 40% of those that have recovered from a disability are *not* working in what they did before (not a new job, a new type of job).   That could happen to you. That is realistic.

What is disability?   Think this through with me.

It could be something related to chemotherapy, a mild stroke, or maybe you are in a situation where you have migraines.

Real example: You have throat cancer and can't speak clearly. How are you going to work? You could be able bodied, but unable to perform your job. Point is, it's not just being laid up in the hospital and being in a situation where you can't do anything.

So, when you are talking about disability income insurance believe it or not the number one reason in America

for bankruptcy and mortgage foreclosures is due to disability, because you don't have enough personal assets to sustain yourself through a period of disability. I'm not talking about for the next 30 years, I'm talking about as little as 18 months.

How much do you have in savings?

How much do you have set aside?

On average, people have a little more than 90 days of funds set aside, tie that in with your retirement and maybe that could last you another six to eight months (and that is straight up most of my clients).

But after that, you are in a situation where you have to clean out all of your assets to continue. Maybe sell your home. It happens fast, believe me!

Why would you want to be in that situation? Here is what I hear every single time. Disability income insurance seems expensive. You know what is more expensive that disability income insurance? Being disabled and not having this insurance. You will spend pennies compared to what would be paid out to you from your disability income insurance.

Why are people so skeptical with disability income insurance?

I'll tell you why, because you think you are invincible.

Let me tell you this, you simply are not. Hopefully that is not surprising to you. Guess what, I'm not invincible either. But we all think that we are.

Think of this, when you get a car, one of the first things you do is acquire car insurance. Am I wrong? Are you planning on getting into a car accident? No. Of course not. But you buy it because if you do get in a car accident, you are covered. Covered for what? Against those risks, and against the risk of having to use other assets to pay your medical bills related and replace or repair your vehicle; not to mention cover others involved in the car accident. Am I right?

Here is another example. If you bought an ATM machine and put it in your backyard, you would agree you'd be a complete idiot if you didn't run out and buy yourself some insurance on the ATM machine.

If I told you I bought an ATM machine, and said to you, but I have it in my backyard, and so I think it will be fine, you would be baffled. Why would you get the insurance? Well, in the event if someone cracks it open, it breaks, gets flooded or anything like that, those risks are covered. But what is the risk? The risk of losing the asset, and the risk of using other assets to replace what was lost. Again, you aren't planning on that happening, but guess what? You still would get the insurance.

Ready for this... you are your family's ATM machine. You are the one that is spitting out money every single day, right? So insure you, and protect your assets, protect your savings, etc. Get yourself disability income insurance; and get the maximum because the maximum is still not enough.

Did you know you can't even buy enough disability income insurance? Pick any insurance company that provides it. Works about the same. They will only allow you to buy 60% of your income to qualify for disability income insurance. So there is no way an insurance salesperson can sell you more than you need, because you can't even buy what you truly need. My great friend Patrick put a spotlight on this fact, which blew me away.

So, stop being skeptical about it and give your insurance advisor a call, ask them for some rates and get yourself some disability income insurance. Right now! And look at the details! If it is cheap and/or didn't require underwriting, most likely it is only going to help you in the most extreme circumstances; which is rare and why it would be cheap and/or require no underwriting. So I am not saying, don't get that. I am saying, be sure you have disability income insurance, not just for the most extreme circumstances.

Here is the thing I want you to mostly focus on. Do not only get what is called "total disability" where basically you must be laid up in bed, unable to do about anything. Make sure it also includes a provision in the policy that covers what is called "partial disability" as well as "catastrophic," which are both additional riders to the policy. Why? Because you are more likely to become partially disabled as compared to totally disabled. And if you have a catastrophic disability, you would want even more to be paid out. Make sense? This is why you must have an insurance professional that specializes in disability income insurance to help get you the best coverage for your situation, needs and lifestyle.

There are all kinds of riders to disability income insurance, but you can also get a rider typically called "own occupation."

This in essence would provide you disability income if you couldn't return to your own occupation, but could work another job. This would make up the difference between what you were making and what you can make at a different job, going forward.

Here is an example. If you are a Doctor and you can't continue to practice medicine, BUT you can teach medicine, this rider (if properly included) would pay you the difference (to the extent of coverage) between what you can make as a teacher and what you were making as a Doctor.

Another example. You are a surgeon who cannot practice again because your hand trembles. Age. Accident. Jammed your hand in a door. Fall down. Slicing an apple.

You name it. A slight hand tremble, and basically you are looking at the end of your career performing surgeries. Apply that to your situation.

So, if you get own occupation you might be able to go and earn a living as a teacher but you'd be in a circumstance where your lifestyle would probably change. However, you could still get some disability income as a teacher because you are not going to make as much as you did when you were a surgeon or a Doctor, if you have the "own occupation" rider. Make sense? So again, apply this concept to your situation.

Insurance Angles

How Do I Calculate How Much Disability Income Insurance I Need?

Did You Know a 3rd Grader Can Do it For You?

JJ THE CPA here. I want to tell you how to basically calculate how much disability income insurance you need. It is simple.

Take what you are making and multiply that by 100%. That is it. That is the amount that you "need." So that is solved.

Guess what? That is NOT how much you can get. You CANNOT buy disability income insurance that will replace 100% of your income.

So how much can you buy? Pretty simple.

Take what you are making and multiply that by 60%.

Boom. Done. That is it.

Now an insurance professional may have some additional analysis to do if your income is variable or you are a business owner; but this should wake you up that you CANNOT replace 100% of your income with disability income insurance.

Guess what else? You could never be sold too much disability income insurance. Right? Think about that. Most think... oh, some insurance salesperson is going to play on my emotions and sell me something I don't really need, and may never use, and probably way too much. WRONG! I told you. Simple!

Oh, you know what else? And this blows me away. Most insurance salespeople, or what I prefer to call insurance professionals, don't really press for clients to get disability income insurance. Why? Because it is too hard to convince you, you need it. Let me clarify something.

If you are working with an insurance professional, not an insurance salesperson, they will insist you consider and most likely require you get disability income insurance. Why? Because they aren't there to sell you. They are there to protect you. So you may have looked at this backwards. If the person you know is always bringing up you buying or buying more disability income insurance, they are most likely not trying to "sell" you anything. They are trying to look out for you. The insurance person that takes no for answer, sells you what you are willing to buy, and then leaves you alone, that's a salesperson.

Wait a minute. What are you telling me JJ? Why won't the insurance companies allow me to buy enough disability income insurance? Ready? Seriously. You ready? The insurance company does not want to provide incentive for you to become disabled or remain, so you do not have to work. They will only pay you 60% of what you make so you will get back to work A.S.A.P.

That is it. No sale required. Why? Because again, you cannot buy enough, and you can't buy what you actually need.

I am repeating this again and again, because it is still a concept so many don't want to grasp the first go around.

Surely you see, you do need it. So contact your insurance professional and get you some. Again, get the max!

Insurance Angles

Do I Really Need That Much Insurance?

Can't I Just be a Cheapskate When Buying Insurance?

JJ THE CPA here. When it comes to insurance, do not just buy cheap. What you want to look at is, that it is as comprehensive as possible.

Right? Don't just think having a particular type of insurance means you are fully covered in that area. For example, you should have some type of auto insurance, but that in itself does not cover any and all types of accidents, damages, etc. Make sense? It most likely will only cover you in the worst of situations.

You probably are going to have to be in a total disaster situation to get any pay out, if you have one of those cheap policies; that costs hardly anything per month in premium. Typically the reason the policy is so cheap, is the insurance company doesn't pay out but in the worst circumstances, which has a much lower probability rate, which allows an insurance company to charge less, because statistically they believe there is an extremely low possibility they will have to pay anything out.

Follow? A cheap premium should tell you there is a low probability of it happening. This is not to say you don't need that coverage too, but you need more than just total disaster insurance. Make sense?

Because disability income insurance is so key, let's take a further look into this area, as we consider the difference between total disaster situations and trying to have comprehensive coverage.

There are several aspects to look at because on some disability insurance policies they will not pay anything until you have hit a 90 to 180-day period of not earning income due to disability. You need to look at when those 90 to 180 days officially starts. Then some policies will only kick in once your income dips to a certain level.
However, by then, it might be too late, and you are in a financial down spiral. There can also be a lot of limitations on what would qualify as disability. Many times a disability that affects your ability to work, is way less that you might think.

It is not always about car wrecks and broken bones. It can be mentally as well as physically, as I discussed before.

Take a minute and just think of all the ways you could become *partially* disabled, that aren't even your fault, and not necessarily freak accidents.

- Get hit by a golf ball.
- Dog bites you on a walk.
- Trip on the ½ inch lip on the sidewalk checking the mail.
- Fall down the stairs going to the restroom during a movie at the theatre.
- Hit by a foul ball at your kid's game.
- Fall off your bike because someone walked in front of you.
- You have repetitive movement at work.
- Moving a friend's couch.

- Slicing your finger making dinner.

- Helping your kiddo get out of the bathtub.

What are some ways you can think of?

Kind of scary, right?

Don't get me wrong, getting cheap disability insurance is better than nothing, but you have not solved anything but the total disaster situation, and cannot even access it unless you are severely or totally disabled.

Cheap is <u>not</u> the name of the game here. Comprehensive is. And yes, it will cost more. Again, think of your auto insurance. If you only get liability, you bet it will be cheaper. But is that the best choice for you. Can't see how it is. And we are just talking about a piece of metal on wheels. Aren't you more valuable than a car? Yes!

Insurance Angels

How Does Insurance Affect My Retirement?

An Angle on Retirement Planning That Will Make Your Head Spin!

JJ the CPA here. Let's talk about retirement planning and how to prepare for retirement. Wait? What? I thought we were talking about insurance. We are. So check this out my friend.

During a tax seminar I taught in Salt Lake City, Utah an interesting conversation came up with a group of CPAs there. It wasn't a new concept, but one that maybe had not been approached before. It was regarding certain kinds of insurances coming into play related to long-term care, disability income and life insurance.

One of the CPAs had said "make the argument for me as to why you would want to worry first about having long-term care insurance and then do you really need disability income insurance if you are trying to save for retirement and/or have assets that you'd be able to use to offset the cost of long-term care or a period of disability?" So, my answer was simple. You would want those insurances from the standpoint of protecting the other assets that you have currently. To avoid using retirement assets. To avoid losing the income that is adding to retirement. Boom! Light bulb came on.

Having insurance allows you to not touch, or reduce your need to use, your other assets when something goes wrong or the unexpected happens.

Simple. Right? Why do you have car insurance? If you wreck your car, can't you just go buy another one? Sure.

How though? From your other assets, right? Your bank account or savings might not have enough, but I bet you could dip into your retirement account for the funds needed. Right? So why do you have car insurance? Because... you don't want to have to do that. You don't want to have to use other funds or assets to replace your car... when you can simply get auto insurance. Oh, once last thought on that. If your car is wrecked. Who pays off your car loan? Who pays off the car loan AND buys you a new car? Yep! See. It isn't only about replacing the car, it is about all the aspects when an accident happens. If you have long-term care insurance and something comes up, a qualifying event, the policy will or should pay for you to go into a facility; according to the provisions in the policy. Seems simple enough. But... remember this, when you are going into a facility for long-term care, it doesn't necessarily mean that you cannot take care of yourself;

what it could mean is that you are needing some assistance because you cannot do everything yourself. On average when someone needs to go into a nursing home it's normally less than two years because it's probably more related to something that has occurred like a surgery or maybe a small stroke. Wait. Have you even considered you might need long-term care not just because you are old?

But why would you want long-term care? Why wouldn't you just say nah, that is never going to happen, so I don't need to worry about it. I have family to look after me and/or I have my assets to use. That is where the above answer comes into play. You should not want to use your other assets.

And, are you sure your wonderful family can look after your special needs for two years, or more? Not smartest choice. Right?

So when the CPA in Salt Lake City asked "why are we buying these insurances if we are saving up for retirement?" It is simple. Because you are trying to protect your retirement assets from being used for anything other than... retirement. Which also includes protecting the income needed in the future to accumulate enough retirement assets. Most of us don't have enough assets for retirement, especially if we are still 5, 10, 20 or 30 years away from it. We need to keep producing income to build up to what we need for retirement, so future income needs to be protected to accomplish that.

Run this general scenario with me on how your income could stop or be reduced, and what happens to your assets and future assets, including retirement assets:

- You become one of the following:
    - Disabled
    - Partially disabled
    - Need long-term care
    - Get in a car accident
    - Dead
- You don't have the proper insurance to cover the event above:
    - Checking account goes to zero
    - Business account goes to zero
    - Savings account goes to zero
    - Retirement account goes to zero
        - You only receive 50%, as 50% went to taxes

- o You start using up your credit cards

- o You borrow money from the bank

- o You borrow money from family

- HOW FAST WOULD THE ABOVE HAPPEN FOR YOU? It's just you, in your own head right now. How fast does all that happen for you?

- You have no assets. You have a ton of debt.

- You start selling assets. Your home.

- IN THE MEANTIME, while your assets have been depleting, and your debt has been increasing, you haven't been able to add anything to your retirement.

- How long will it take you to recover all the money, retirement and assets, pay off all the credit cards, banks and family to just be back to break-even, and then how far are you behind on saving for retirement.

- Dang! Right?

Having proper insurance at the proper coverage protects your assets and retirement assets. So having insurance absolutely needs to be a part of your retirement planning. You can save maximum retirement dollars for 25 years, and it all be gone in a year, without proper insurance to protect it.

Insurance Angles

Business Insurance is Boring!

Can't I Worry About it Later?

JJ THE CPA here. Whether you are starting a business or been in business for a while, here is what I want you to stop and evaluate.

What kind of insurances do you need as a business owner? Don't guess. Know!

There are so many different kinds of insurance for businesses, and most of the time there's not one kind that you don't need. Therefore, what probably would make sense is to evaluate how much do you need of each kind of insurance, and when is it appropriate to get the insurance.

So, for example, if you are a new manufacturer you may not need to run out and get a 10 million-dollar policy, if you haven't even sold your first product. What you might need is that same insurance but maybe you need to get it to where there's a million-dollar product liability protection, with the ability to get up to the 10 million-dollar policy as your grow.

Do know this, there are certain insurances that you need no matter what.

I want you to note, I am not going to cover every kind of insurance you need as a business owner. That would be a whole other book. Probably several. What I want to open your eyes to are the insurances I tell my clients to look at, get and have.

And to peak your interest in getting with your insurance professional(s) to do a comprehensive look at what insurances you should have, and ensure you have them... and enough.

So, what we are looking at here is when you are in business and you have employees you first and foremost are going to need work compensation insurance. That is so if your employee gets injured you have insurance to cover not only their injuries but cover their payroll during their time off. It is insurance that you want to get, as it benefits not only your employee, but also your business from having to pay all that out yourself. Some states require it. Also, the type of business you have affects what you need, based on the potential risks you are asking your employees to take with their job. A secretary risks falling down the stairs at your office; and that is no joke.

The other aspect to look at is any kind of liability. If you have a location that employees, customers or just about anybody that is coming on to your property, whether you are renting or owning, you want to have some general liability insurance. Say somebody trips and falls or any other kind of injury that's going to happen, you are in a situation where you have insurance that is going to cover that; cover the injuries and all related.

The other thing you want to look at is that if you have any assets in your business, (computers, furniture, equipment, vehicles, etc.), you want to make sure that you have insurance to cover (replace) your assets.

The other aspect to look at is having life insurance. You want to have life insurance obviously for your heirs, but wouldn't it be good to have life insurance that would at least cover and pay off any business debts that you have?

If you have a business partner, you would want to have life insurance that would be able to come into play to buy out their share of the business and pay for the affect to the business through the death benefit.

If you are in a situation where it is just you primarily generating the revenue of that business or its primarily relying on you, you would want to have disability income insurance. Why? So, if something happens to you, since you are the ATM machine for that business, you'd want there to be a continued amount of revenue now <u>not</u> coming from the business but coming from your policy to cover your personal income needs.

If you are in a situation where you have a key employee, you might want to have life insurance and disability income insurance on them for the same kind of protections for you. Pay them while they are out or pay something to the family if they pass and pay something to your business to aid in that time of absence or replacement. Which is better for you and your business? You pay that or the insurance company pays for it.

What about business overhead expenses? What is that? Overhead expenses are expenses that you are going to have no matter if you show up or not. So, what would happen if you can't show up? What is going to happen if your key employees can't show up because of sickness? What about an ailment that prevents you from being able to work? There is business overhead insurance for those very reasons. It is insurance that pays out... to cover your overhead expenses, while you or a key employee can't continue generating income for your business.

There are also types of insurance that if you get a loan it's just comes in play to pay off the loan, if something were to happen to you; disability or death.

Health insurance. This isn't necessarily required for all small businesses with a small group of employees. Small businesses can be classified differently by separate definitions, depending where you are located in the U.S. You would want to look at getting health insurance for yourself, of course, but you are not automatically required to provide health insurance for your employees. However, you would want to make sure though that they have this insurance available to them.

Get them the connections. Why? So if they are in need of medical services, they can get it paid for; not you (out of the kindness of your heart).

Here is what I recommend, whether starting a business or you've been in business for a while, <u>evaluate</u>. Go over the following with your insurance advisors:

- What insurances do you have?

- What insurances do you need?

- Do you have enough of each kind?

- Are you in a situation where you have too much of one?

Insurance professionals that are truly professionals are not going to necessarily lead you astray. An insurance professional may put you in a situation where they are going to want to make sure you are getting the most possible. Why? Because that's their job. They're going to tell you the worst-case scenario. You just started your business, here's why you need $10 million dollars in product liability, and you are going to spend $25,000 on an annual premium... but have not built one thing. You might hear "If you build one and now you are selling it, what if the first one creates a disaster." Maybe that insurance professional is correct, but there does have to be some sense of reasonableness of when you are getting it and how much is appropriate. So that insurance professional may be correct, but not for another year or ten down the road. Make sense?

Also, depending on your budget, while you want to make sure you have enough insurance, you want to also ensure you have *all* the different kinds of insurances needed.

So, going to your insurance professional first may not be the best way to keep everybody in check. Who I would check with first, is your attorney because they are the ones that are going to either be the one suing or defending, not necessarily even you, but they are going to be the first ones to know what you need to protect your business and yourself. The question to ask an attorney isn't necessarily, what insurances do I need. The question is what type of insurance should I have, *no matter what*?

Then talk with your banker. Why? The banker is obviously going to want to protect themselves, as well as you. They are going to lead you in the right direction, because first they do not want you to buy too much of insurance. Why?

Because they want to make sure you have enough cash flow. They are also going to make sure that they are looking at the risks to insure against so they are repaid, even in the event of disaster, so the bank will look at the same kind of risks that you'd be looking at. So that is why a bank might have some good suggestions.

Finally, talk with your CPA. Say hey, what kind of insurances do you feel that I would need as a business owner and hopefully the CPA is going to give you the types that you need. Why? Because they should already be working with business owners, and based on experience, they will have some great ideas, potentially. More importantly they will help tell you how much you need in this regard or here's what you don't need.

Meaning, a home-based business would most likely not need business overhead insurance; because there is no real additional overhead to cover. Make sense? Now don't get me wrong, a lawyer, a banker and a CPA are not going to want to be in the position to tell you, oh you only need $500,000 of this or $25,000 of that. Why? What are you going to do if something happens and that wasn't enough? You are going to go to those professionals and say gosh darn it, you didn't tell me to get enough? So we are not going to give you a definitive number typically and that's where you rely on the insurance professionals to help and guide you on how much you need, but by knowing that your lawyer, banker and CPA/EA have been involved in giving you some ideas of what types of insurances you need.

Now when you are with insurance professional a lot of what is going to come into play is what? Your budget. Because when you sit down with the insurance professional they are going to show you $38,000 worth of annual premium and you may need exactly what that insurance professional is recommending to you; however, if you just started out do you need to spend $38,000 annually or can you? If you've been in business for 2 years would that then make sense? If you've been in business for a long time, maybe you know some other professionals in the insurance industry that might be able to give you a different quote or a different opinion. Maybe you have too much of one kind of insurance you need to reduce and get more of another.

Here's my point, there's really not many insurances out there that are a waste of your time to *consider*.

What can be a waste is having too much or too little of something; or just not having any of it. So with that being said, definitely do a review of your insurances and on an annual basis. Take a look of what you have and visit with the professionals around you to get their opinion.

Since we are talking about figuring out how much insurance you need. If you are working with someone that is trying to sell you something based on emotions, run. Emotions may convince you need the insurance. But emotions don't determine how much. With any kind of insurance, you can always "calculate" how much you need. And so if the person who is selling you insurance can't show the calculation of how much you need, then by golly, demand they show you. And if they can't or won't, run. You may be thinking, how does JJ know there is a calculation to knowing how much insurance I need, on any kind of insurance? I know this because every insurance company out there calculates how much you need, as they don't want to pay out more than they have to, which is largely based on what you actually need. If you have a $45,000 vehicle, no auto insurance company is going to insure your vehicle for $90,000. Make sense?

Emotions convince you need it. A calculation shows you how much. This also makes it much easier to ensure you aren't being over sold based on your emotions, because if someone plays on your emotions, and you are then convinced you need that insurance, a proper calculation would show you, you don't need any. Follow? You bet you do!

Insurance Angles

What if my partner becomes disabled?

How does that affect me?

JJ THE CPA here. Imagine this. You have a business partner and they become disabled. You are going to be in a situation where you've gone into business with somebody, so they must be like family, if not closer. Now you and your partner, or partners, have a business together, and of course you know when you own a business you are absolutely invincible: nothing will ever happen to any of you. Right? You all are made of steel! Everything is going to go great until you retire and everything will just work perfect and magically…right?

Here's the crazy thing, I had not been presented this concept until a few years ago when I started looking at insurance in regard to protecting my clients and their assets, and if they find themselves in a situation where one of their partners becomes disabled what are they going to do? This was a scary wake up call, that no one is talking about.

There is disability income insurance, however that just protects income of the person with the disability. *Really hear this. Don't skip ahead.* What happens though if your business partner becomes disabled to where they can't continue to help with the business because they cannot work, or their assets are depleted so they can no longer sign off on notes or put capital in?

I know right off the bat there will be people reading this thinking, well you know that's like my brother or sister that I'm in business with and I'll take care of them forever. Okay, that's all fine and good when you are making a speech to yourself in the mirror, and I am not saying you wouldn't. However, wouldn't it be better to have some insurance in place that would just take care of the effect on the business? And better than you or your business could afford, for potentially pennies on the hundred dollars that it would cost to actually do this.

Also, there is just the reality. Let's just say you have a dental practice and there is two of you, (and of course you would always want to look out for your partner), but now there's not two dentists, there's one.

How will you have the money to really support you and your family AND your partner and their family in their permanent disability? Again, I'm not talking about the partial disability that would prevent them from continuing to work for a period of time. I am talking permanent disability where it prevents your partner from being able to produce or participate, whether it's physically, mentally or financially.

There are a lot of circumstances and as well-intentioned as we all are, there are just circumstances that are beyond everybody's control, and then it comes down to this.

I, the partner who is not disabled, have to move out of my house, downgrade my lifestyle and go deeper into debt because I want to help my partner.

And maybe you would do that, right?

For the next five, ten, fifteen or thirty years, depending on where you are in the life of your business. So I guess it does make sense not to spend $48 a month because you'd rather just go ahead and sell your house and tell your kids you can't pay for their college because something happened to your partner and you do want to see that commitment through, but it's not worth spending $48 a month. Of course, I am being sarcastic. But guess what? I hear this all the time.

Pause for a minute. If this happens, at some point, and sooner than you think, it will be either you and your family, or your partner and their family. Seriously, sit in your own thoughts, in your own head, there will be a point you wouldn't be able to sustain supporting this circumstance.

And then... how will you feel when you look your business partner in the eye, and their family, and say, I am so very sorry, it is not possible for me to keep this up, or at least not to the extent they need. Now, wipe that image away, and imagine before depleting assets, downgrading and borrowing money, you present your business partner and their family a huge check to pay them for the business, ON TOP of their disability income. Boom!

It's kind of ridiculous right? You don't plan to get in an auto accident, so of course you don't waste money buying auto insurance. You don't expect anything to happen to your house so no need for homeowner's insurance either. Of course, I'm being extremely sarcastic. No one buys car insurance and walks out and says, sweet I am going to get into an accident at year end and get all my money back!

No one thinks about this. Everyone thinks its crap and that it's just another salesperson trying to make a commission. Wrong. The reason I find it irritating and what makes me the most frustrated about this, is that this is a huge problem for any business that has a partner. Any business that has a specialty, and an employee that you are very reliant on. You have a business and you are doing research and you are relying on that one person to do and continue the research, or that spectacular salesperson. The point is that you can get disability insurance that buys out your partner so if they become disabled you can buy them out. I'm not talking about for $50,000 which might be all that you can afford on your own or even a $150,000, if you were pulling from your assets. I am talking about for fair market value of their portion of the business. So if you are really doing things the way that JJ the CPA would have you do it, you would have disability income insurance on your partner and yourself, and in addition to that, a disability buyout policy so that if you have a partner or you yourself gets disabled, you AND your partner are covered. Boom!

Insurance Angles

Is There More Than One Kind of Business Related Insurance?

JJ THE CPA here. I want to talk to you overall about business related insurance and why it's important to make sure you have all the different kinds, depending on the type and size of your business. I know I am beating a dead horse (as they say in Oklahoma), but I really want to change the way you think about insurance.

When you get a car, you go buy insurance immediately; don't even think about it. If you bought a $10,000 watch, I'm sure you bought insurance on it. If you bought a house, you get insurance on it.

So hopefully with the same thinking, you personally have life insurance as well as disability income insurance.

You are the most valuable asset you have. I would assume since you bought this book and you are reading it, that this would be a concept that you'd agree with.

But if you own a business, the most troubling things that can happen to it, even before you consider losing clients or the like, is if something happens to you, if something happens to one of your employees or if something affects your businesses liability. I'm not necessarily talking about tornados; your general liability insurance policy hopefully covers those types of things. I'm talking about things that can come into play the causes a disruption to your business, other than shutting it down.

Do you want something that's going to affect your business for 90 to 120 days to then cause your business to go out of business? I'm telling you right now, most small business do not have enough money sitting in their bank account to last 90 days; plus collectible accounts receivable. Having the proper business insurances will save you from depleting operating funds; which affects the financial strength of your business.

If something happens and depletes business operating funds, how quickly would your business need to close? How are you going to generate income if your business is closed? Do not sit around thinking you are a super hero, even though we all do, me included. Don't think that you are not going to need certain types of business insurance. Especially if you are in a business in the service industry which is reliant on labor; you included.

Insurance Angles

I Have Auto Insurance, So Aren't I Covered?

The Secret to Learn From Having Auto Insurance!

JJ THE CPA here. Let's talk about your auto insurance. Why? Because when's the last time you reviewed it? Do you have the key provisions that your insurance agent would recommend to you?

Most of the time the insurance agent isn't going to necessarily recommend stuff just to make more commission, because in the auto industry the commission aren't necessarily that great. What you want to be paying attention to is, what do you need if anything goes wrong, because most likely an experienced auto insurance agent has seen it all.

There are many different riders with auto insurance. One of those is uninsured (under-insured) motorist. With uninsured motorist, that simply means that if you get in the car accident and the person that you were in an accident with doesn't have any insurance or doesn't have enough insurance, then your own insurance company is going to come into play and make sure that you are taken care of; whether it's related to property, medical, lost wages, liability, etc.

You want to be in a situation where you are fully protected and you are already totally open to the idea of auto insurance, as I no one would need to talk you into that. Right? So why aren't you looking at your life insurance? Why aren't you looking at disability income insurance?

If you have it, great! Make sure you have enough of those insurances as well, so you are not uninsured or under-insured, in the same manner with your automobile.

Did you catch how I used auto insurance to look at other insurances in the same way? Of course you did.

Insurance Angles

Why is Buying Life Insurance so Emotional?

Buying Life Insurance is Not an Emotional Decision. Period!

JJ THE CPA here. Let's talk about why buying life insurance is not an emotional decision.

First, you are going to pass away. The only question is when. So having life insurance is a guarantee pay out, as long as you have it in place when you pass away. It may be emotional to think of passing away, and the effect on those left behind, but it should NOT be an emotional decision on getting life insurance, or getting the amount your heirs need.

If you are being pressed to buy life insurance, and its being told to you in an emotional way, please just take a step back. All that is a scare tactic to get you to buy life insurance. And one of two things will happen if you continue down that road. You will buy more than you want to ease your emotion in the moment, but may cancel it later; or, make the insurance salesperson go away, and don't buy any. Don't try to make the pain of buying life insurance go away. See it as a calculation and the pain will go away on its own.

Life insurance is a must. You know that. So stop being emotional about. Stop thinking of it as leaving a lottery ticket for someone, and you aren't sure you want them to have more than they need. No widow has ever said, there was too much death benefit.

When you pass away, you know you would want your loved ones to have plenty of what they need. Not just right up to the line of what they need. Stop over thinking this. It's only an excuse. And if you think you can't afford it, that's typically only an excuse to have more for yourself now, and less for your loved ones later, because you don't want to give something up now. You may think, JJ how could make such a statement. However, if you don't have enough life insurance, most likely that is exactly what you are doing. Own it.

But I guarantee, to the person reading this, you do not have enough life insurance because I have yet to work with a client that had enough when I reviewed it with them. Personally, I do not even have enough. However, that is because I had a health issue in the past that has prevented me from getting more; so I am stuck.

So how do you know how much life insurance you need? Let me turn you thinking around. The amount of life insurance YOU need, is how much YOU need if your spouse, loved one, partner or business partner passed away.

When we hear, how much life insurance do you need, think, how much do those left behind need if you pass away. Make sense? Here we go. Using round figures, follow this simple calculation of three things to find out how much life insurance you actually need.

* How much debt do you have?

*How much do you live on a month? Multiply this amount by 200.

*What legacy amounts do you want to leave behind?

Add those 3 things together. BOOM! That is how much life insurance you need. And you better be rounding up!

If you pass away, you would want your heirs to be debt free. Why? Simple. The assets will be free and clear of any kind of debt.

Secondly, thanks to my great friend, Matt, who shared this with me... "the rule of 200;" best shown with an example.

If you live on $10,000 a month, take that number and multiply it by 200. That is 2 million dollars. (They don't call me JJ the CPA for nothing.) Then if you take 2 million dollars and multiply that by 6%, which is an average of what can be made on invested money, that will generate $10,000 a month in income.

By doing this, your heirs should not have to touch the principal, which alleviates the concern of when the nest egg would run out. Make sense? If you don't leave enough, your heirs will have to use the principal to make ends meet, and with less principal there is less that can be earned. And at some point, the principal runs out. Not good!

Lastly, what legacy amounts do you want to leave behind? That is above and beyond paying off debt and the monthly expenses. Many might say if my loved ones that are left behind have no debt, then they do not need as much each month. Okay, great. Wait, really? There is no inflation? Hot water heaters never go out? If the money runs out, people can get a job or another job? Yes, I am being sarcastic. But it's because I hear these excuses all the time.

That same good friend Matt has shared that the one thing NOT ONE widow or widower will ever say is, "I got paid out too much life insurance."

MOST IMPORTANT:

Again, life insurance on you, is not for you. It's for the ones that you are leaving behind. When you are calculating how much you need, you need to include the person who is actually going to use the life insurance. Make sense?

Insurance Angles

I Don't Think I Need That Much Life Insurance.

Life Insurance Is NOT For You!

So, Who Are You Buying Life Insurance For?

JJ THE CPA here. In the previous chapter we briefly discussed this, but I feel it is so important to talk about this, it deserves its own chapter.

Many times, over my career I have had this discussion with clients, and I tell them repeatedly, you are not buying life insurance for yourself.

Life insurance is for the people that you are leaving behind. For those that you are naming as the beneficiaries. So when you are deciding how much you should budget to spend on premiums for life insurance, do not think about what you have to give up. Instead, think if something happens to you, what will your loved ones have to give up, if they don't have enough life insurance paid out to them. Think about that when you are thinking about how much life insurance you need to leave behind for your loved ones. Then, while the premium cost is for sure a consideration, you will better know how to budget for it.

Follow me for a minute. True story.

In 2007 I got a call from a client's wife and father informing me my client, her husband and his son, had died. I was the 3rd person the father called and the 5th person the wife called. My friend and client had passed away just hours before the calls. He left behind a young wife and 2 small girls. I can stop there because you should have enough of an image in your mind to fully digest that

LIFE INSURANCE IS NOT FOR YOU.

Let me repeat this. Nothing about getting life insurance is about you. It is about the ones that are being left behind. So, when deciding how much life insurance you need or want to buy? That is a conversation you need to have with the ones you are leaving behind because it is about their life, how they continue to live and I hate to say it, it then has nothing to do with you.

That is it.

It is pretty simple then. Right?

I harp on this because it still is something I have to repeat to clients over and over; even the ones that understood this initially; they have to reminded.

Insurance Angles

Like Auto Insurance, I Can Get Life Insurance Anytime I Want, Right?

JJ THE CPA here. Now that we know why you need life insurance and we know who you are buying life insurance for, like I shared before, you most likely do not have enough life insurance currently. Right now, as you read this, there is a 99% chance you do not have enough life insurance. How do I know? Because no one does, me included. I know you might not want to hear that, but it's a reality. Did you know getting life insurance can be hard? If you have medical issues you may not get any, like me. You may not qualify because of family history. I have a client, a healthy person, that finally decided to get life insurance, only to be turned away because of family history. Are you worried now? Keep reading.

When getting life insurance, the earlier in life that you can get it the better because it is cheaper. Family history will always be prevalent, but your medical issues may not. I know you might be young, fit, and healthy now, but what about in 5, 10, 15 or 20 years when this starts to become more important to you? It may be too late for you to get enough coverage that you can afford or qualify for, to take care of the ones that you are leaving behind.

By doing the simple calculation that was provided to you in a previous chapter you can better protect your loved ones. So, look up what you currently have in life insurance, do the simple calculation and call your insurance professional and get fully protected.

Know that with life insurance, you can get different terms and different amounts for each term. If you get a 10 year term policy, it will typically be cheaper than a 20 year term policy.

Why?

Because the insurance company is only going to guarantee your premium and coverage for 10 years, which is less risk for the insurance company. There is more risk for the insurance company to cover you for 20 years, because, you guessed it, there is longer period of time the insurance company will pay out a death benefit if you pass away.

So for the insurance company to do this, they need to charge a higher premium. Why mention this? If you get a 10 year term policy, what happens in 10 years? You will need to get insurance again, which means you will have to go through underwriting again, which means, you will be re-evaluated. Your health, your finances, your family history, etc. And you will be, you guessed it again, 10 years older. All that equates very easily to even higher premiums, even if you get another 10 year term policy. Why? Because you are now that much closer to passing away, which is higher risk for the insurance company, which requires higher premiums.

With all that being said, when actually buying the amount of life insurance you need, consider how much you need for the various phases in your life. What are the ages of your kids? How far are you from retirement? How old is your spouse? You most likely need more now, then you will need later. So, don't necessarily look at getting one policy for a shorter a period of time, so you can afford the insurance you need now. Consider getting multiple policies to cover the amount of life insurance your heirs need, based on where they are in life. Stated simply, you can have a 10 year policy, a 20 year policy AND a 30 year policy. All different amounts, all covering your heirs differently at the phase they will be in life. And locking into it all now will be overall less expensive because you got it younger. Follow?

Get what you need. Which means, get what your heirs need. Make yourself afford it, because I bet you can.

Insurance Angles

Isn't the Life Insurance Provided by My Employer Enough?

JJ THE CPA here. When you are looking at your life insurance to determine how much you need; you really should not count the life insurance you have at work. It is a wonderful benefit if your employer offers it, especially if they are going to pay for it. Obviously, you should take advantage of it. If you are a part of a group plan (which is fairly standard), you can get some very inexpensive life insurance through your employer. If so, yes, get it; and get the max. Many times, though, that group life insurance is going to be $50,000 or two to three times your salary.

Here is the thing to know, that is not enough.

Period. Remember the calculation that we have talked about in previous chapters. I guarantee you that none of you came up with only needing $50,000 in life insurance.

You will need life insurance whenever you pass away. However, most term life insurance is only offered until around the age of 65; or if you get some lasting past then, it starts to get pretty expensive.

Take this into consideration, are you going to be with that employer much after age 65. Most likely not. In this day of age, people are switching jobs, and you don't want to put yourself in a situation to where your family's life insurance protection that is contingent on you having that job with that employer. Meaning, you are not going to get enough life insurance through your employer and if you ever separate from that employer you will not have that life insurance anyhow.

So, you need to have life insurance outside of your employer and you need to have much more than $50,000 or two to three times your salary. You need to follow the simple three step calculation I shared with you to determine how much life insurance you need, without counting what you have at work. And, you need to further consider you most likely won't have much of any term life insurance much past the age of 65.

Insurance Angles

What is the Differences Between Term and Whole Life Insurance?

JJ THE CPA here. What are the differences between term and whole life insurance? The biggest difference between them is that term life insurance ends, well before you statistically could die. Whole life insurance, sometimes called permanent life insurance, does not have an expiration date. You will have whole/permanent life insurance no matter how old you are when you die. Most term life insurance policies will end when you turn 65, or if you bought a 20-year term life insurance policy at age 35, then it would expire when you turn 55; and so on.

When it comes to the cost difference, let's think about this. Most likely you not going to die before age 65. Most likely if you have a 20-year term policy, you are not going to pass away before it expires. What is guaranteed though, is you will die one day. With term life insurance, the cost is going to be less than whole/permanent life insurance because the life insurance company is rolling the dice that you are *not* going to die before age 65, or the end of the term. With whole life insurance, the insurance company knows that they will pay out a death benefit no matter what because you will die one day. This why whole life insurance is going to be more expensive than term because it will always be around for your heirs.

Here are things you want to look at with your insurance professional related to whole (permanent) life insurance.

1. Does the death benefit with whole life insurance go up each year?

2. Is there a dividend paid each year and how much?

3. Is there guaranteed growth of the cash value?

4. What is the policy loan rate if you borrow from the cash value?

In considering the above, the other key benefit to whole life insurance is that it can build up cash value. I will say this, not all houses are built the same when it comes to cash value so that is something you really want to look at carefully with your life insurance professional. Once you know the above, here is few ways on how to apply that knowledge.

1. What will the guaranteed cash value be, as that will determine what you can borrow from the policy, while you are still alive.

2. If you borrow from the policy, you want to know the policy loan rate because you want to compare that to the guaranteed growth to determine the differential, and also compare the policy loan rate to the historical dividend to also see the differential. Why? Because you want to ensure that as you borrow money from the policy, if you don't pay the interest on that loan, the cash value will grow larger than the interest expense added. This all to avoid the policy imploding. How does a policy implode? You owe more to the policy, than the cash value. If you don't pay down the loan, the policy closes so the cash value can be used to pay off the loan. Implosion means there will be no death benefit.

3. You want to know if the death benefit grows because as you borrow from the cash value of the insurance policy, you want to ensure there is enough

death benefit to pay the loan off when you or the insured passes away. If the amount owed to the policy exceeds the death benefit, the policy will also implode, if the loan is not paid down. Again, implosion means there will be no death benefit.

Here is the takeaway, while you are young get as much term life insurance that you can (and need) because that is when you typically have the most risk to reduce; having younger children for example.

Then once you get enough term life insurance, you want to look at getting whole life insurance so you can make sure you have something left behind when you pass. Again, its ensuring you have the proper amount of life insurance for the different phases of life. And, like term life insurance, the younger you can get whole life insurance the better as it relates to premium cost; which should be lower than if you got it when you were older. Also, the younger you get it, the more time there is to build up cash value, that can potentially be used by you, during your lifetime.

Again, get with your insurance professional on this. There is much to consider, like anything else. Buying whole life insurance should really not be an emotional decision. It is an economic decision, typically part of your overall financial plan. With that being said, watch for the signs if you have an insurance salesperson or insurance professional helping you with this. Remember what I shared before, and insurance professional should be showing you the calculations.

Something to note, most CPAs are not fans of whole life insurance. I am, with the right company.

If a CPA is not a fan, they most likely are not considering it properly, and are only thinking of the cost of premiums. While you may want to include your CPA in the decision making process, if they are an automatic "no," you may need to ignore that as this is not really their area of expertise, and because they shouldn't be a "no" on whole life insurance, in general.

Attorneys that deal with estate planning, typically are fans of whole life insurance because they deal with the *death* aspect of the planning, and having death benefit, no matter the age someone passes, should always be of benefit to the heirs they are left working with.

No matter the professional on your team you involve with this decision, if they can't tell you why you shouldn't get whole life insurance from the "calculation" perspective, and only a hearsay or emotional response, then you may need to take their suggestion on this with a grain of salt. Your professionals on your team, should not be making emotional decisions ever. Their job is to be objective, which requires... looking at the calculations to generate an opinion.

One way to know if a whole life policy is a good one, is to look at the company that is issuing the whole life policy; and ensuring they specialize in whole life insurance.

As I stated in my opening to this book, you need to deal with those that specialize in what you need. I won't mention companies here, but there really are only a handful of life insurance companies that really specialize in whole life insurance. And those companies that do, have been providing whole life insurance for a very, very long time, with a good track record of policies not imploding. An insurance company that designs a whole life insurance policy properly will do it in a manner that it should not implode, unless you go outside the lines of how it was designed.

A good whole life insurance policy is one with a death benefit that grows, with guaranteed cash value growth, a good historical dividend and a policy loan rate historically less than the dividend. All of this information can be found when researching the company; similar to how you would research a company you would consider investing in. Whole life insurance is not an investment, but determining which company to get a whole life insurance policy with can be approached in a similar matter.

Insurance Angles

Is Whole Life Insurance an Investment?

JJ THE CPA here. I want to talk to you about why you need to make sure you are not seeing whole life insurance the same as any other investment. It is not an investment. Now in your mind you might think it's an investment and you may misclassify it as an investment, but let me repeat, it is not.

Why is it so important for you to know this? An investment is typically money going into a market or a business. An investment is typically something that does not have any guarantees. When you are talking about insurance, you have guarantees. What are some of the basic guarantees you would have with whole life insurance? You can have a guaranteed amount of premium and death benefit. This is assuming you are not going into an universal policy or a policy tied to the market; which I do not recommend because life insurance is not an investment and if tied to the market, if affects its guarantees. If you are with the right company you are going to have a guarantee of increased cash value, and your death benefit will be guaranteed, with possible increases.

When you put money in the market or into an investment it does not have those guarantees; not that I can think of or have ever seen. I am not advocating in any way that you should ignore the market and only put money in life insurance. You need to be well diversified. What I am advocating is do not see them as the same thing. They are not. Many people will say, when they fully grasp the concept of whole life insurance, I want to pull my money from the market and put it in whole life insurance. While there are countless factors to consider, it would make sense you have money in the market, invested in a manner consistent with your risk tolerances and proper diversification. This is where you need your team involved, to help you find the right balance.

What you need to do is evaluate what you need investments for, and what you need life insurance for. While there is overlap, they are for different purposes. The most obvious is, life insurance is first for *after* you pass away, even if you have a policy with cash value. See what I am saying?

Bottom line stop thinking whole life insurance is a scam. If you do, you probably are thinking that because you are thinking of whole life insurance as an investment.

It is not. Stop thinking of life insurance the way your grandparents described it to you because it is just not that way with policies being issued today. Whole life insurance can play a huge part in retirement planning, as well as with your legacy, but it's not an investment.

Insurance Angles

Should I Consider Whole Life Insurance as a Part of My Retirement?

JJ THE CPA here. I was at a conference and this discussion came up regarding the use of whole life insurance for retirement. I want to focus in on one aspect of that, assuming you get the right whole life insurance, you are now in a situation that when retirement comes, you should be able to access the cash value inside the policy, tax free. How? Policy Loans.

A policy loan is money that is pulled from a whole life policy tax-free.

How is it tax free? Because it is a loan. Loans are not taxable.

Why is that important?

Because typically you do not have to take as much risk to grow it to a higher amount to pull in retirement as compared to a taxable account.

What?

When you pull money from a (qualified) retirement account that is taxable. So you have to have more in that account because you aren't going to get what you pull out: you are going to get what is left after you pay the tax on that.

Okay? Stay with me.

So if you pull out money that is not taxable, you don't have to have as much, because you don't have to hold back (pay) taxes out of what you pulled out.

Huh?

You have to have more cash value in a taxable retirement account to net the same amount as what you could pull out from a whole life policy. Taxable vs. Tax-free.

I am not following you JJ.

Try this. If you have $1,500,000 in a taxable retirement account, that is really approximately $1,000,000 to you, after tax, depending on your tax rate, etc. So having $1,000,000 cash value in a whole life policy would be considered the same as having $1,500,000 in a taxable retirement account. Again, this based on a rounded average with more assumptions I could shake a stick at, but you get the point.

Makes sense JJ. So what?

So, don't look at the *growth* of cash value in a whole life policy as the same thing as the growth in a taxable retirement account.

Whole life insurance is not an ugly thing. You do want to be careful that you are picking the right kind of policy with the right company, just like anything else in this world.

Insurance Angles

If I Have Disability Income Insurance, Should I get a Disability Rider on My Life Insurance Policy?

JJ THE CPA here. Let's talk about the rider on life insurance typically called the disability rider. This is a smart rider to get in most circumstances because if you become disabled and you are not able to pay the premiums, the rider will kick in and pay the life insurance premiums for you.

The worst thing that could happen is you are hit with a severe disability, even if its temporary, and you can't continue to afford the premiums on your life insurance policy, and you have to cancel it. So, a disability rider kicks in and starts making your premium payments for you, which is an extremely smart decision especially if you have a high premium that would need to be paid.

If you got life insurance later in life and your premiums are $200-$500 a month, please see how much more a rider would be. There is not a standard percentage of the premium that rider would cost because too many variables come into play. However, I will say this, no matter what you are paying for that rider it will be a great benefit it something happens to you to keep your family well protected.

Insurance Angles

Isn't Life Insurance on My Kids Just Wrong? Isn't it Just the Rich That Do This?

JJ THE CPA here. Are you a horrible parent? Do you hate your children? Those would be the parents that refuse to get life insurance on their kids. I am kidding. Well, not entirely.

You should and can get life insurance on your children. I get it, I would never buy life insurance on my children with the mindset that they may die before me; no parent thinks that way. I want to outlive my children and I do not want to receive a death benefit from them.

BUT YOU DO NOT GET LIFE INSURANCE ON YOUR KIDS FOR YOU!

YOU GET LIFE INSURANCE ON YOUR KIDS FOR YOUR KID'S HEIRS, YOUR GRANDKIDS.

YOU GET LIFE INSURANCE ON YOUR KIDS BECAUSE THEY MAY NOT QUALIFY FOR IT LATER IN LIFE, OR WHEN THEY DECIDE TO GET IT FOR THEMSELVES.

ONCE YOUR KIDS BECOME OF AGE OR MARRIED, ETC. YOU CAN TRANSFER OWNERSHIP OF THE POLICY TO THEM, AND THEY CAN SELECT THE BENEFICIARIES.

IN ESSENCE, YOU ARE LOCKING IN LIFE INSURANCE "FOR" YOUR KID, WHEN IT IS CHEAPER AND TYPICALLY EASIER TO BE APPROVED.

WHY IS THIS IN ALL CAPs?

BECAUSE YOU NEED TO THINK DIFFERENTLY ABOUT LIFE INSURANCE ON YOUR KIDS. THE RICH. THE SUPER RICH SEEM TO DO THIS ALL THE TIME. THE RICH GET RICHER. AND THIS IS ONE WAY THEY DO.

Your kids are going to grow up, possibly go to college, maybe get married and even have children. Yes, one day unfortunately they will pass away. When that happens, they will have loved ones they are leaving behind.

So why would you get life insurance on your children?

Simplest answer, they may not be able to get it later in their lifetime.

Why?

You do not just automatically get life insurance because you filled out an application. You must be in good health. You must be in good enough health that the life insurance company does not think you are going to die any time soon.

Life insurance companies are there to make money. That does not mean that they are bad, but they are rolling the dice that you are not going to die. Why? Because then they do not have to pay out. This does not in any way mean that life insurance is a rip off. What it means is that the life insurance company hopes you live. Therefore, they are not going to approve life insurance, or as much, on people with medical issues. So, while your children are young, you can lock into an insurance premium rate at let's say 18 years old. So, when you child turns 18 let's say you got a 20- or 30-year term policy. They will then have that same premium up until age 48 at most. Think about everything your child will do in those 30 years. By the time they are 48 they are most likely going to be married with children themselves, as well as a mortgage and other responsibilities. You would have provided and/or obtained something that will help protect them through that all.

What happens if they reach age 30 and then have health issues and cannot get life insurance?

What a genius and best parent thing to do for your children; buying them life insurance at a young age.

Think of it this way, you are and your child is not benefiting from this. Who is? Your grandchildren. So, by you buying life insurance for your child at graduation, you are buying protection for your future grandchildren. Boom!

BUSINESS

NUMBERS

ENTREPRENEURS

IRS

DEDUCTIONS

S CORP

ADVICE

TIPS

NAME

SMALL BUSINESS

ENTITY

C CORP

VEHICLE

STRUCTURE   LLC

SECRETS

ACCOUNTING

Business Tips, Secrets

I Need to Name My Business Before I Can Start a New Business, Right?

JJ THE CPA here. When you are starting a new business the biggest hurdle that so many must overcome, just to start, is finding that perfect name to your business.

I want to tell you one thing about that. It does not matter when it comes to the legal structure, and what I mean by that is that when you go to Secretary of State in whatever state you are in to formalize your business legally, it can be whatever name you want. Whatever name you choose, does not have to be the name of the business on the signage out front, because that's just the legal entity name.

You can typically use a DBA (Doing Business As) by either just doing business as such or go to the Secretary State and file a DBA report. Usually it is cheap, and then you would own that DBA. By doing this, you protect the name. NOTE: If you don't file your DBA with the Secretary of State, then you don't own it and a competitor can start using it, and possibly own it, if they file the DBA with the Secretary of State. (Some states may have another department to file that with. An attorney in your state should know.)

Many business owners get really caught up in this and before they even open the doors, they're thinking, I really have to have the name "Goliath LLC" because we're going to be so successful and we're going to have competitors that will be coming for us, and when we go nationwide we need to make sure we protect the name.

Well, if you haven't even started, if you don't even have a bank account opened yet, if you don't even have a client, then relax... you don't need to worry about the name as much as you think, at this time.

What is key is, just get the business started, and then maybe the "perfect" name will come to you later.

Maybe you already have the name but now you are concerned about how to get it structured for tax purposes. None of that matters when you go to Secretary of State, as all they really care about is one thing: what's the name of the business, and then there's some other questions to go along with it. Meaning, you are setting up the business for legal purposes at the Secretary of State, not for tax purposes or even for the signage out front. You are not deciding when you go to the Secretary of State, what's my tax election, should I have two bank accounts, where should my office be, where should I lease; none of that matters to get your business born legally. The quicker you can get filed with the Secretary of State and pick a name for the legal structure, like X7499, LLC – GREAT! Then as you get your businesses going you can file a DBA. There are a lot of businesses that have multiple streams of income and so they might have multiple entity (DBA) names, but it's all owned by the same business, by the same company. Follow?

What I am encouraging you on is… just get it set up and get going. Don't be frozen because you can't come up with the perfect business name.

NOTE: When you file with the Secretary of State your business name is only protected in that state. So don't get ahead of yourself and try to figure out how you protect your name nationwide, when you haven't even really started. The best way to protect your name nationwide is to do a trademark once you have that business name in place and you feel good about it. But here's the thing, don't get ahead of yourself and hire a trademark lawyer and go spend $10,000 trying to protect the name when you haven't even done anything yet.

Here is my recommendation.

Get started.

Get past the name issue and get started.

Business Tips, Secrets

I'm Starting a Business, So What Do I Need to Know?

JJ THE CPA here. I want to bring you some general knowledge as it relates to things when you start a new business.

So many people ask, will I get a checking account? Should I get a credit card? Yes, to both.

You do want to get a checking account. However, that checking account should only be for business. It cannot also be both your personal and business checkbook.

I know that sometimes you think well it's just so much easier if I can just pay my mortgage, pay my kids tuition or that quick run to the grocery store out of my business account. The problem with that is that if you are running personal expenses through your business, if you get into any kind of lawsuit you have given impression to those that are suing you, the attorney, that you are really not a business; and then they can possibly pierce the corporate veil and go after personal assets. Another problem with that is the IRS could come in and say, you are not a business, from the standpoint of being a S-Corp, C-Corp or Partnership. The IRS will look at all these personal expenses you are running through, and they may collapse your entity for tax purposes and you would owe additional tax that would be related to that; with penalties and interest added. Another reason to have a separate bank account is so that you really know what's going on in your business.

A lot of small businesses get a little bit too focused on what money is left over; the daily balance in their bank account.

What you need to really look at is:

What am I collecting?

What am I spending?

What is left over?

Then you are paying attention to what is it that you are pulling out for yourself.

It's easy to get yourself in a situation where you get confused and you think, I am only pulling out a thousand a month for myself. Well, are you really? Maybe you are only pulling out one thousand to yourself, but you are running two to five thousand of personal expenses through the business. If so, your business is paying you more than you may think. Also, by having a separate bank account for your business, it really gives you a better sense of what the business is doing. I get it that you may want to look at your daily balance to figure out how much money you have in your business account, why not. But if you are running personal expenses through, you don't really have a true sense of how much money is actually available for the business and its needs. Make sense?

The other aspect of having a separate business account is to better protect you from the standpoint of those that are not owners. I'm not necessarily saying that your spouse is going to do anything or even your employees, but you want to have that separated out to protect your asset.

As it relates to a credit card, a lot of people want to get excited, confused or overwhelmed and think "I have to get a credit card in the business name." That is not the case. That is not how it has to work. You can charge on a personal credit card account and then the business pays for it. The key is, you would only use that personal credit card for business purposes; or only have your business pay the portion of the credit card balance for business expenses.

The reason to have a separate bank account and then a separate credit card is so you are separating out your expenses. If you have a credit card and you are running personal and business expenses on it, then it's going to be a little bit harder for you to figure out what is what when it comes time to pay it; how much is business and how much is personal. I know that in the beginning you could say, well I will always know that. Well, okay. But once you get busy, it's not going to be as easy as you think. So, what is better, is to have a separate credit card for business expenses and then have your business pay for them. There is going to be times when you are out and about having a business lunch or need to buy something at the office supply store. So why not have a separate credit card to buy it.

The other aspect to be thinking about is when you have a bank account you can also have a debit card. So same thing applies with that. You only want to be using that for business purposes. Then you are in a situation where not only do you know better what your business is doing, you know better its cash flow. You know the money that's left over is actually for the business, and you are protecting yourself in the case of a lawsuit or the IRS collapsing your business and causing you to pay additional taxes.

I know it sounds basic, and you are right it is. And having separate bank accounts and credit cards actually keeps it basic.

Trust me.

NOTE: When you go to open a business bank account, most of the time the bank is going to want to see the Articles of Incorporation, the certificate from the Secretary of State, to show that you are legally set up. They're also going to want to see paperwork showing that you have a tax ID number; which you will receive when you apply for it. When you go to get the tax ID number, it would be great to have your CPA get that tax ID number because they will ensure you get a copy of the letter that allows you to prove your EIN; in essence the social security number for your business. With that the bank is also going to want to see your operating agreement (LLCs, LLPs or the like) or by-laws (corporations). This not only shows who the owners are, but the details of who is responsible for the liabilities and assets of the business, who is managing the entity, etc. It does not matter if you are the only owner, they are going to want to see an operating agreement or the by-laws.

Business Tip, Secrets

What Tax Classification Should My Business Be?

JJ THE CPA here. What we are going to talk about now is, what kind of tax classification should your business be.

I want to first focus on differentiating between the legal entity and the tax classification, or really what is the tax classification. Many people, and I'm even talking about attorneys and CPAs, still get confused by this very issue.

When you go to the Secretary of State, you are going to set up your legal entity. It is not there that you then select if you are going to be an S-Corp, a Partnership or a C-Corp. That is only something you can elect with the Internal Revenue Service. Period.

What you are going to do with the Secretary of State is just set up your business. You are going to formalize it, make it legal and give birth to it. That is where, as discussed in a previous chapter, you are going to give it a name and indicate who the registered agent is, which simply tells the public who to contact if there's any reason to contact the business or its owners.

You do need to decide how you need to be set up for tax purposes. Are you are going to be classified as a C-Corp, S-Corp, Partnership, Sole Proprietorship or even what is called a disregarded entity. You want to know that before you go to the Secretary of State, so you don't want to choose an entity that possibly cannot be classified as you need with the IRS and/or your state.

So, know how you want to be taxed, and then match the legal entity type with that.

This will require some coordination with your attorney and CPA or EA. If these professionals are experienced in your industry and business type, it should be easy for them to decide with you.

With all that being said, here is the thing I want you to focus in on, and I don't care who you are, these are two separate issues. Legal formation and tax classification. Do not let your attorney tell you how it should be taxed, or tell you it doesn't really matter. As wonderful as attorneys are, my experience is they can be arrogant when it comes to setting up a new business. The attorney that makes decisions about how to set it up for tax purposes and obtains your EIN without checking with your CPA (even if they are a tax attorney), I say, please stop it! Here is the thing, the lawyer sets you up legally and they are done.

They need to figure out what kind of entity you should be for liability protection and legal purposes. But, the kind of business you are going to be on the legal side can determine how you will be classified on the tax side. That's why the CPA should communicate to your lawyer how your business is going to be classified for tax purposes. Then that lawyer's job is to take that information and recommend the type of entity you should be for legal purposes. The lawyers are doing a great job, but their job is to put together a business entity that protects you, shields you, help you figure out who the owners are, what happens if your business implodes, sells, if your partners or other shareholders retire, die or want out, etc. That's what you want the lawyer figuring out with you. They are not figuring out how you going to be taxed. They are not figuring your financials, signing your tax return or anything that's going to be dealt with year after year after year after year. Yes, they might deal with lawsuits, but that is not every single year; hopefully.

So when you are getting with a CPA and you are figuring out the tax classification, that is completely separate and you don't need to figure all that out by yourself.

Before you do any of it, come up with the most general named possible so you can get started with your CPA. Say here's the kind of business I'm going to have, they will ask you a series of questions, how many owners? How big will it be? Of course, everybody's going to say, it's going to be the biggest company in the United States of America working to make 58 million dollars in our first year!

You are going to answer some realistic questions with them that will help determine the best way for it to be taxed.

How do you know it's the best way to be taxed? If it leads to you paying the least amount of tax.

So, do you want attorney coming up with your tax entity status as well as the elections and getting your tax ID number? Unless they are your CPA and they are going to do your tax returns every single year, get with your CPA.

Early in my career I met with a client, who already got with her lawyer and paid him $1,500 and they were set up as an LLC, and at the time in my state the LLC could only be a partnership or C-Corp; which was a long time ago.
I sat down with her and I showed them how the kind of business they were going to be in (computer consulting) they really want to be classified as an S- Corp for tax purposes as it's going to save 15.3% in taxes every single year they are in business.

If they net $100,000 and are in business for 20 years, it is going to save $300,000. You know what the client said? I mean well, we just dealt with this lawyer, and already paid $1,500. I said, well go back to that attorney and tell them they should have checked with a CPA first, and fix it.

Overall, check first with your CPA to determine your tax classification and then get with your attorney to get it legally set up.

Business Tips, Secrets

What is My Business Structure?

JJ THE CPA here. When you are setting up a new business or have an existing business you should to review your structure. If you have been around awhile, know this, things have changed. Bottom line, you want to make sure that you are taxed in the most advantageous way, which leads to paying the least amount of tax.

For my CPA practice, there's really two main tax classifications I work with. One is a partnership, which files of Form 1065, the other is an S-Corporation that files at Form 1120S. The biggest difference between the two: A partnership has to have a second owner, and is best designed for the type of activities and/or investments that you are <u>not</u> actively involved with. Primarily this would be real estate activities or your direct investments into *other* investments. Done this way, when you are paying tax on the net income down at the individual level you will not pay self-employment tax, up to 15.3%; which is an extra tax on top of your individual income taxes.

When you file the partnership return (Form 1065), if it's from activities that you are involved with, as in you are literally making the business run, you have the risk of having to pay self-employment taxes; no fun.

When you have an S-Corp, you file Form 1120S, and with that you do not pay that self-employment tax on the net income. You would just pay regular income taxes on the net income. However, the catch with an S-corporation is you need to pay yourself reasonable wages, which there's quite an opinion out there as it relates what reasonable wages are.

If you are sole proprietorship, that is typically a side hustle or small, small home-based business, with the net income subject to self-employment tax.

If you are C-corp, the entity pays tax on its net income, and the owners pay tax on the wages and dividends they received. If you are disregarded entity, you simply file the income and expenses on whatever tax return that wholly owns it. The term disregarded in this situation simply means it doesn't file a separate tax return.

Business Tip, Secrets

Why Do I Need to Look at My Financials? Because if You Know Your Numbers, You Know Your Business!

JJ the CPA here.   Know your numbers. I hear a lot business owners say they know their numbers because they look at their cash balance every day. They say they know what's going in the bank and what's going out. That's probably a pretty good exercise so that you know what's in the bank, but here's the thing, you might know what went in, but are you really going to remember what went in last week, last month or this time last year?

The money that's going out the door when looking at your daily banking activity, is just based on when something is clearing your bank. It doesn't mean that when it clears your bank that's when the expense was incurred.

It doesn't even mean that is when the expense was paid. If you are only looking at your bank balance when you are logging in, you really don't know your numbers other than maybe in about of 48 to 72-hour period. What you want to know is your numbers when you get to financial statements because you will be able to see your numbers broken out by categories and over a specific period of time.

How do you really know your numbers? Look at your financial statements. What is that really? A balance sheet and profit & loss statement.

A balance sheet is simply a list of your assets and liabilities as of a specific date. The difference between the two amounts is your equity.

Equity doesn't necessarily mean that is what your business is worth, but it tells how much your assets exceed your liabilities, or vice-versa.

A profit & loss statement is your income and expenses, to arrive at a net profit or loss.

Go get your last set of financial statements. Like real quick. Doesn't even matter if they are 2 years old. The concepts I share here are timeless.

Now, look at your balance sheet! Sometimes this can be called "Statement of Assets, Liabilities & Equity."

Look at your assets. You want to know how much money you have in the bank, this amount should take into account what hasn't hit your bank account.

If you are looking at your balance every morning, that is great, what it won't reflect what hasn't cleared.

Do you have accounts receivable (A/R)? This is what's to be collected. Accounts receivable should be cash getting ready to go in the bank, once collected.

What are your other assets? As it relates to the strength of your company, whether that's hard assets or inventory, you will see those balances as of that date. So now you can see the available assets that can further your business.

Now, look at your liabilities. You have a credit card, a line of credit, loan and/or a note payable. The reason you want to be aware that is so you have a clear picture of what you owe. Easy, right?

What is important is you really want your total assets to be more than your total liabilities, so that you have positive equity.

What's going to happen with your liabilities? You must pay them off. That is going to use up cash to then reduce your liabilities.

The reason you want to be aware of that is when you've got cash going out the door for expenses, you need to make sure you have enough left over to pay off debt and vice-versa. That's your first glimpse into cash flow management, which is what makes or breaks any business.

Now when you go to your profit and loss statement, you need to know what did you collect? What did you spend? The difference... you guessed it, your profit or loss. Seems simple enough. However, there are two different ways, or accounting basis, that you need to be aware of that determines your profit and loss.

There's accrual basis and there's cash basis.

When you are looking at your profit and loss statement on the cash basis, which is what I recommend, you are seeing what was actually collected and what actually paid.

When looking at an accrual-basis profit and loss statement, you can really fool yourself on how your business is doing, because it doesn't take into account what was actually collected or actually paid. It takes into account when income was earned and expenses were incurred. The biggest reason this can fool you is you may have billed lots of clients, but collected little. You won't know this when looking at your profit and loss statement on the accrual basis.

So even if you have the ability to have accrual basis financials, you absolutely must look at your cash basis profit and loss statement to really know your numbers. I like cash basis because cash is where the rubber meets the road. So when you are looking at your gross sales, that is the gross income you've actually collected. Then when you look at your cost of goods sold and expenses, that is what you've actually spent.

Some additional items to note about your profit and loss statement: Costs of goods sold are more based on how much business you do, so they're variable. Your overhead expenses are typically fixed; in essence you will have those expenses whether you open the doors or not.

Your net income... This has an interesting relationship to your available bank balance. Focus in with me. Alot of people look at their profit and loss and say, "I netted $100,000, so why don't I have $100,000 in the bank?" That is where we want to look at your cash flow statement, because it will show you that relationship. Here is your net income but a cash flow statement shows where money went that didn't go on your P&L. What? This would have been dollars to pay off debt or pay distribution or dividends to owners. So, this shows the relationship of your net income to what's in your bank account because it takes your net income and lists the additional monies used or added to arrive at your available bank balance.

You want to know your numbers because as The Profit, Marcus, from CNBC says, "If you know your numbers, you know your business."

Business Tips, Secrets

Isn't Accounting the Same as Bookkeeping?

JJ THE CPA here. Let's talk about accounting and what that means.

There is accounting and then there is bookkeeping. Bookkeeping is part of accounting, so when we are talking about an accounting system, we are not just talking about the entry into the accounting software or into QuickBooks which is what most small businesses use. When we're talking about accounting, we are talking about a system. We're talking about the controls to safeguard your assets, safeguard the deposits of the money that's coming in and safeguard the money that's going out; check writing and credit cards.

When we are talking about an accounting system, what we want to look at is deposits and expenses. Now if you are in a position to where it's just you doing all of this or you have your spouse helping you, you might not need to do all of this. However, once you get big enough, like my practice, and you have some people helping you, you need an accounting system.

Safeguarding money coming in. Put yourself in a situation where, like in my firm, I have one specific person who checks the mail every day. They are the one that slices the mail open, and if there are any checks or payments to us, immediately flips it over and stamps it payable to us.
That way it is only going to get deposited into my business bank account. Then that is taken to the bank to deposit.
Then someone different will go into our QuickBooks and record those deposits paid against the invoices.

That is an accounting system.

Safeguarding money going out. The other part of my accounting system is that I have another person that I give invoices to and then that individual is the one that's writing the checks out for expenses. I am looking at it first, when the mail comes and is sorted. I am the one giving those expenses or those invoices that need to be paid to the person that is actually going to write the checks, and then I am the <u>only one</u> that has a signature authority. I'm the only one. Then when those checks are coming back to me to sign, they have an invoice along with it, and then I'm the one that signs the check; catch my drift. And I'm the one that puts it into the envelope and seals it. Then it gets mailed out. That is an accounting system my friends. Safeguarding revenue.

Another part of an accounting system is getting the invoices out to your client, however you do that. So for me, I have somebody else that's involved, that they're the ones that are creating the invoices and making sure they're getting mailed out. Then I'm the one that's also making sure if they're getting mailed out, so we have collections. So I am keeping an eye on it. That is an accounting system.

Accounting is not just the bookkeeping part because if you noticed that wasn't even really until the end. Money coming in and how to safeguard it, money going out how to safeguard it, ensuring that what's being paid is what you want to be paid, invoicing and how to get that out the door, that is all a system, right. It truly isn't that complicated. Just come up with a system that involves at least couple of people helping you, and most importantly involves you.

If you only have one other person in the business, then you should be the one that is still looking at the bank statement every month. You should be the one that's only signing the checks. You should be the one that's only taking the deposit to the bank or at least periodically, so its unpredictable. The bottom line is, be aware of an accounting system but don't overwhelm yourself and think that is so complicated you just throw your hands up. It's not. If it is, you probably are making it harder on yourself than it needs to be. They key is to stay involved and separate out the various duties.

Business Tip, Secrets

What is the Difference Between Cash & Accrual?

JJ the CPA here. Let's talk about the difference between accrual and cash. I shared some about this in a previous chapter, but only as it relates to your profit and loss statement.

On your financial statements it makes a huge difference, in terms of what you are looking at when it comes to either cash or accrual basis.

With accrual it has nothing to do with what you actually paid, or what you received. What am I talking about? If does not matter if you have written a check and paid a vendor. Doesn't matter if you paid your employees in the sense of having money leave your bank account. With accrual it doesn't matter how much you deposited, because on accrual basis it is simply how much have you invoiced your client as that is your revenue for the month on the accrual basis.

So, you may have collected nothing, but billed your clients $1,000,000. Your P&L is going to show on the accrual basis of accounting $1,000,000 of revenue, even though you didn't collect a dime, but that's the revenue on the accrual basis. Now let's say to generate that $1,000,000 of revenue you incurred expenses. To keep it simple, let's say that you are a business that buys supplies to then resell them, and you have to pay the labor to do it. So, let's just say in that same month the amount of goods that you had to buy plus labor was $700,000. However, for grins let's also say you haven't actually paid anyone yet. With this example, you would show on accrual financials, you netted $300,000. So you can sit there and go, wow this is a great company how can I invest, they must be doing wonderful, or how can I loan them money? See the trouble here. This is why accrual financials, in my opinion, are the worst thing to look at when you are looking to invest in a company, or make a loan to it.

When you are looking at the strength of a company you want to look at the cash basis, because in this example, which is real life, no money came in and no money went out, but it showed a $300,000 profit. However, on cash basis for that month it would be a big fat zero income, zero expense, and netted zero.

So, let's just say, in that same month you collected $400,000 and you spent that $600,000 on goods, overhead and labor. On cash basis financials, you actually spent $600,000, you actually collected $400,000 and you had a $200,000 loss.

When you are looking at cash basis financials you show a $200,000 loss. If you are looking at an accrual set of financials, you are showing $300,000 net income. That is a differential of a half of a million dollars. Now what are you thinking?

It can be tempting when using accrual basis to fudge a little. How? Put in invoices to your customers that you've sold, but maybe you haven't sold all the way, or bills you've received but you wait to enter them in.

See the danger? The danger is you will have financials that are based on when you *feel* the activity should be recorded and aren't based on what is actually being collected and actually being spent. The fudging is usually to make yourself or the business owner feel better about their numbers. Numbers don't have feelings, right. So cash basis removes that by being based on reality.

The first thing we asked when we're looking at anybody's financial statements is, is it accrual or cash? If they say accrual, we ask for cash. Why? Because that's where the rubber meets the road. It's for real what was collected, for real what was deposited and for real, what's left in the bank.

With your balance sheet, sometimes call Statement of Assets, Liabilities & Equity, the biggest difference is with cash basis, it does not reflect your accounts receivables or accounts payable. The reason is because cash basis financials are based on what was collected and spent, not based on what was billed or what is owed. Therefore, only on the accrual basis financials will you see receivables and payables. I discuss these items in the next chapter. Giddy up!

Business Tips, Secrets

What's the Relationship Between Accounts Payable & Accounts Receivable?

JJ the CPA here. Let's talk about the relationship between accounts payable and accounts receivable. These are both found on your balance sheet on the accrual basis.

Accounts receivable (A/R) is basically what you invoiced the client that you haven't been paid yet; you haven't collected it. This should be the number one focus of your activities, in your business. These are services that you've provided, and/or goods that you have sold. The client owes you and you need to get paid. Period.

A lot of times with small business owners they get caught up on the next job, taking care of the client that's asking them to do something today. However, your businesses life blood is money coming in and a big part of that is accounts receivable. When you are looking at accounts receivable you need to make sure that everything is in there; it's complete. If you've done the work, bill it and collect it. Period.

The other aspect of A/R is knowing how it compares to what it normally is. So you have to be looking at your A/R often to know what is normal. You want to compare it to last month and the same month in the last 2 years. How does it compare? Meaning, if you normally have $100,000 in accounts receivable and it's sitting at $60,000, that is going to tell you a couple of things.

One, you may have done work that hasn't been billed to the client yet, so that needs to be addressed ASAP. Or, two, maybe you've done a great job of collecting but guess what if you are normally at a $100K and you are for real at a much lower amount, this should tell you that less will be coming in as you move forward; and to prepare accordingly.

Here's one of the most important parts of comparing A/R and accounts payable (A/P). Accounts receivable should always exceed your accounts payable. Why? Accounts receivable states, here are things that you've done that you haven't been paid on. The accounts payable is the opposite. It states things that have been done for you or sold to you, that you haven't paid for yet.

How are you going to pay those payables?

I know that you can look at your bank balance and say well, I am going to pay it out of my account JJ. Great, but typically if you have receivables and payables, the relationship between the two is that you want those receivables to be able to pay off the payables. Future income to pay future payables due. So that is why it is important to know and have accurate figures. If you are in the opposite, A/P is higher than A/R, then you know you are going to have some cash flow problems coming up. Meaning if you owe more to vendors than you have coming in from clients, you should know that your future cash flow has some issues and you need to get busy on getting money in the door with new projects and collecting from those that owe you. That's why it's also important with your accounts payable to make sure that it's accurate. Do not fool yourself. What is it that you owe and put it in there. I am not saying you would put in twelve months of future rent, however, what should be in there on April 30th is the rent that's due on May 1st and possibly due June 1st.

Be aware of what it is that you owe to vendors to make sure that you have the cash coming in from your receivables to pay off those vendors.

Accounts receivables is what you are billing customers in the ordinary course of business, and accounts payable are those vendors that you owe in the normal ordinary course of business. So ensuring your A/R exceeds your A/P helps ensure you are looking at future profits, as these are what is expected to occur with your cash flow in the near future.

Business Tips, Secrets

What Bookkeeping Software Should I Use?

JJ THE CPA here. Let's talk about what I recommend for the bookkeeping software, for you and your small business. QuickBooks. Period. The end.

What I recommend before that is you hire a professional bookkeeper and have your CPA involved. The best company I know is CPA Enterprises, P.C. owned by Justin McAuliffe, CPA aka CPA JMac! (I don't do bookkeeping services.)

However, you most likely need to do the entering expenses yourself, cutting your checks, entering in your deposits, if you want the best use of your bookkeeping activities.

And with most small businesses, that will be done by you, your spouse or a trusted employee; that's just reality. Either way, you want your CPA to be aware of what is going into your numbers. Why? So they will prepare your tax return in the best manner possible; which means in a proper way of paying the least amount of tax.

As of the date of the publishing of this book in 2019, I only recommend QuickBooks desktop version, and do NOT recommend you use QuickBooks online or the app. You want to buy the CD and install it on your computers. If you have a Mac computer, you need to buy a PC and use it for QuickBooks. Bookkeeping is one of the most important aspects of your business, as you don't know your business, if you don't know your numbers. This is not an area to do what is popular or cheap or even convenient. You do your bookkeeping right, and I believe you give your business double the chances of being in business next year.

All other accounting programs are terrible. Period. The end.

I work with a variety of small businesses, and they, we, all use QuickBooks. Remember, now a small business is up to $25 million gross. Doesn't matter when it comes to using QuickBooks. I have worked with many companies that are larger than that and they are using QuickBooks.

QuickBooks is meant for the non-accountant, which means it's meant for you as the business owner.
The beauty of QuickBooks is that you really can focus on just what it is that you need with your financial statements.

If you are in a situation where you are going to do your own QuickBooks, go find a local college or trade institute and just take a 3-hour class on it. You don't need to know everything about QuickBooks to get rolling. It is easy enough that you can just Google something or go to YouTube to just learn the basics of anything else. Even if you can't take a class, use QuickBooks. Not Quicken; that's personal expense tracking only. Use QuickBooks.

The biggest aspect of it is you can just go to the check register and it's just like you entering numbers in a paper check register, from back in the day. You just enter in the date, check number, who you paid and the dollar amount. The only difference between QuickBooks and that good old-fashioned paper check register is that you are going to pick an "account" to associate with the item. When picking an account, it's not a magic trick. It's not turning water into wine. It's basically taking your general knowledge to know that if you went to Office Depot you would pick the office supplies account, or if you pay rent to a landlord you would pick the rent account. That's really the only scary part to QuickBooks; picking an account.

As it relates to the most basic function, here's what QuickBooks does beautifully; it kicks out financial statements. Financial statements being the balance sheet and the profit and loss statement. What's great about this is even if it's a simple little mom-and-pop, sole proprietorship, QuickBooks is a great fit for that.

If you are a 25-million-dollar company and you have lots of clients, inventory, payroll, accounts receivable, accounts payable and you need accrual and cash, QuickBooks is your best bet for that.

Here is what you want to focus in on. I mean it. Hear me right now. Listen to what I'm getting ready to tell you, right now. Your financials, that you are going to hand to your CPA, even if they're looking through it, are used to prepare your tax returns. Do you want to be hell-bent on using some software that your uncle told you about, that is free or do you want to be in the software that your CPA convinced you of.

If you are using some other software and it's producing financials, there is a good chance, in my 26 years of experience, those financials from another software is going to cost you tax. Let me repeat that, you do not want to have a software that's going to produce financials that is going to cost you tax. What do I mean by cost you tax?

I mean you are going to pay more money then you need to because the financial statements will not best reflect your cash basis or accrual basis activities.

We have brought on new clients using another accounting system and many were overstating their income. What is overstating income? That means they were reporting income that they had not received, or it was doubled up and they were paying more tax than they needed to.

Let's focus in on one thing here. The biggest expense you are going to have in everything you deal with it, is taxes.

What you can do about it?

Get yourself with a good CPA; a great one. You want someone that is good at looking at your numbers. But wait, even as good as they are, if they get crap financials, or you just give them a P&L, how do they know those numbers are good if they have no details? The reason I will only work with clients that are using QuickBooks is that we know how to look at the detail to figure out things like, has income been doubled. It is so simple, but income can be inflated on your financials and you wouldn't even know it.

Again, QuickBooks is the way to go because of one very simple reason. It gives you the best chance of producing financial statements that will be best for tax and banking purposes. Why? Because QuickBooks is all-encompassing. If you have inventory, payroll, accounts payable and accounts receivable, it can handle it.

Again, it's meant for the non-accountant.

Business Tips, Secrets

What is My Tax Structure?

JJ THE CPA here. Let's talk about tax structure. In a separate chapter, I talked about setting up your entity at the Secretary of State and how that really has nothing to do with your tax classification. So let's expand our discussion on tax classifications.

What are tax classifications? C-Corp, S-Corp, partnership, disregarded entity or sole proprietor. Done.

All of these can be an LLC under current law. That is why the LLC has become the easiest choice for the legal set up. With an LLC, there's a Form 8832 that makes electing your tax classification with the check of the right boxes.

Now it may look simple but get with your CPA or EA so they can prepare it and get it filed. Filing this tells the IRS, I set up an LLC and now I would like it to be taxed as _____ (check the box). There are deadlines to when this needs to be filed. Another reason to get with your CPA or EA.

When you are looking at what kind of tax classification your business should be, here are rules of thumb in very general terms.

With a C-Corporation, this would most likely be a fit for multiple owners with a business that is expected to grow quickly and you want to have stock. With a C-Corp it pays its own tax, which immediately you may think that's exciting, but at the same time if you own the company either you are paying tax or the company's paying the tax.

Either way, tax is being paid, and affects how much you put in your pocket as the owner. You may also think with the corporate tax rate being less than the individual tax rate (as is the case under current law in 2019), it would make sense to have a C-Corp. However, with a C-Corp double taxation comes into play. Now that may not matter if you are in a situation that you have a lot of owners and you think you are going to sell it. Maybe there is a situation where you want the business entity to pay tax, and with a C-Corp, that is the case.

If you are more of a one, two or three owner type business (closely held), then the S-Corporation or Partnership can be a good fit. The biggest aspect to be aware of with both is neither pay tax at the business level but whatever the net income is, the individual owners pay the tax on it, for Federal tax purposes. Not what money was pulled out.

Whatever the net income is, that is what the owners pay tax on.

For those that are going to be active in the business, actively managing the business and/or a business that provides a service, the S-Corp most likely is your best route because by Statute the net income is not subject to self-employment taxes; a 15.3% tax in addition to regular income taxes.

If you are going to be active in the business, actively managing the business and/or a business that provides a service, and you are taxed as a partnership, the net income WILL BE subject to self-employment taxes; a 15.3% tax in addition to regular income taxes. Seems pretty simple right? Active involvement or a service business, elect to be taxed as an S-Corp.

So why would anyone want to be a partnership? Because S-Corps need to pay its owners payroll for their services. Payroll is subject to social security and Medicare taxes, which is the same tax included in self-employment taxes. Also, if you are getting into real estate or passive investments, meaning you are not going to be active in the business, the partnership is really the best way to go from the standpoint of the partnership being easy to get assets in and out, with the ability to have multiple types of owners with different types of ownership percentages.

So why would you want to be an S-Corp if I have to pay wages to yourself, and pay payroll taxes instead of, but the same as, self-employment taxes. Because the owner can pull distributions (like dividends but not double taxed) that are not subject to payroll or self-employment taxes. So the tax savings are experienced on the savings of self-employment or payroll taxes.

There is no regular income tax savings between an S-Corp or a partnership, for Federal tax purposes.

So... JJ the CPA... what the heck?

If you are going to be active in the business or in the service industry, the S-Corp is the most favorable for Federal tax purposes. If you are not going to be active, the partnership is the most favorable for Federal tax purposes.

You can be a sole proprietorship if you are just doing a side hustle or starting a business to see if it will work. You can, but you don't have to get an EIN for this entity, or formalize it with the Secretary of State or the IRS. You don't have to have a separate bank account. But if you start making money, you want to change your classification as this tax classification has the downfall of paying self-employment taxes on whatever it nets, which is an additional 15.3% in taxes.

You can formalize an LLC that is classified for tax purposes as a disregarded entity. All that means is that it doesn't file a separate tax return. This is most prevalent in real estate investment activities.

It may be advantageous to have each real estate property owned by a separate LLC for legal and liability protection purposes, but filing a tax return for each and every property could be unreasonable. Therefore, you can structure an LLC to be wholly owned by you (one person) or your business, where all the activity is reported by you or the business. From a tax standpoint, there is no extra savings with a disregarded entity tax classification. It is effective to reduce the number of tax returns to file, and consolidate the activity into less tax returns.

Business Tips, Secrets

When Should I Have a Buy-Sell Agreement?

JJ THE CPA here. Let's talk about buy-sell agreements for businesses. One of the things that we want to look at is the unfortunate time when someone passes away that owns part of a business.

Do you know what happens when a business owner passes away? Their estate owns their portion of the business. Now whoever is remaining, they are now partners/owners with the estate, which means they are now partners/owners with the beneficiaries of the estate, which most of the time is the family; the spouse and children (possibly grown). Not saying that is a bad thing but it would be a much better situation if there was a buy-sell agreement in place if this happens, and even better if there could be funds immediately available to buy out that partner (the estate & beneficiaries) so that the estate, the heirs, spouse or whoever's left behind is able to get a good value for the business and that family can then benefit monetarily from that.

I know that there's a lot of opportunity where businesses may continue and someone may be a silent owner/partner so to speak and maybe the surviving family would continue to own that. Again, that might be possible with a very big business, but most of us are small businesses and so if one of the owners/partners passes away, it's probably pretty monumental from the standpoint of now there's that lost effort of the deceased owner/partner. There is that lost mind, so to speak, that's helping run the business, solve problems, sell, work, etc.

Now, if you think your business could be in a situation where even if the business can continue to pay out that estate/heirs/surviving spouse/family something similar to what the deceased owner was making, most of the time the estate and heirs are going to still want fair market value for the business. Follow?

Then the remaining owner(s) of a business that's left behind is not going to necessarily have the money to continue to pay out regular income and/or pay out the value of the business to the estate/heirs. Right? Could that business even borrow money to do that? Would the bank loan money to a business, if a key owner passed away and all that value and effort ceased as well.

Let me be frank with you, if you can't be honest with this situation, it's going to be pretty rare if not near impossible to make that happen. And even if a surviving business owner made it happen, out of honor and loyalty, what shape, what financial state is that business in, after the payout? Take any small business, I don't know any that I have ever worked with that would have the funds on hand to be able to buy out the deceased partners share of the business.

Now what happens when a buyout can't happen? Then you get into a situation where now there could be bad blood over it, so to speak. Now negativity of money comes into play. I know everybody right now is getting along in the business. You were cooking out at a barbecue last week and everyone had so much love for each other; and everything is just going grand. And then I'm sure you would never think you wouldn't have your fellow owners back.

Why? Because all the spouses and kids love each other, and your business is all about family. Right? You bet it is! You bet you are sincere when you look your business partner in the eye and say, "if anything happens to you, I go you. I got your family." And you absolutely mean it, and believe it. But there is simply reality of available resources.

So the fellow business partner has passed. There are obligations that have to be taken care of on all sides; the deceased family, your family and the business. So why not have some agreements in place on how it's going to be handled; which includes how will the estate will be paid out, when and at what amount and/or value. That leads to the most important aspect of a buy-sell agreement, which is funding it. Meaning, how will the surviving business owner(s) be able to pay for the buy-sell agreement in the event of death, taking all the considerations into account.

Simplest answer is... having life insurance in place so that you are able to benefit the remaining heirs, immediately by the way, and then you as the surviving business owner are going to benefit because you are using the same life insurance proceeds to buy out the family; to pay for the buy-sell agreement, or fund it. I know "buyout" sounds like "screw them over" because absent the owner passing away, that specific owner would still own the business. So the remaining family could feel if they are getting bought out, it is somehow a negative thing.

However, with the leverage of life insurance, that's not the case at all, because it's the best chance at giving the estate, the surviving spouse, family and heirs the best or most value on the business. Otherwise I don't know how you, in reality, get that paid for and/or how quickly you could make that happen. Furthermore, a buy-sell agreement tells the deceased partner's family they agreed to the buy-out in the event of their death; which solves all kinds of problems and heartache.

Now, you may just continue to be an owner, and if you don't have money to buy now, that's okay. You can just continue and you will now have the beneficiaries helping you run the business. You'll have to somehow figure that out. But again, with many small businesses the only money being paid out is wages to the owner, and there isn't necessarily a ton of profits leftover. Right? Why?

Because profits just go back into the business or pay off loans and/or a line of credit.

So now if you have a business that is going to continue, and it doesn't have money to buy out the surviving heirs, and the owner that passed away was only making a "wage." And... the reason they were getting paid a "wage" is because they were "working" and "earning" it. Now you have a business owner that was "working" in the business, but now you have to replace that person and you probably are not going to be able to replace them with anybody that could truly replace them, in terms of all the value they brought to the table as an owner. There's now going to be some effect to the revenue (if the owner was a part of that process) and the expenses, I would assume, which leads to an effect on the financials that the bank and possibly other investors will be looking at. So, again, life insurance would be a great thing to have in place, with a buy-sell agreement also in place so that if a business owner passes away, the business can continue, the buyout can occur as pre-planned, including a plan on determining the value and most importantly, be funded, and immediately paid.

So don't wait. Get life insurance in place, and a buy-sell agreement. You want an insurance professional and your attorney coordinating together on this. Do not cut corners and ask or let your insurance professional put together the buy-sell agreement for you.

Business Tips, Secrets

What is the Difference Between Profit and Gross Profit?

JJ THE CPA here. Let's talk about the difference between profit and *gross* profit, and why it's important to you. NOTE: THE LAST SENTENCE IN THIS CHAPTER IS THE MOST IMPORTANT BUT FOLLOW ME THROUGH THIS JOURNEY THROUGH YOUR PROFIT AND LOSS STATEMENT TO ANSWER THIS QUESTION.

If you own a business, everybody's interested in what the profit is. Well, what I would first be interested in is what's the gross profit. Once you grasp the terminology and how each is calculated, which you may already get, be sure to read what I, as a CPA, look at when advising clients, because you most likely will be very excited on what you will be able to do with this information.

Gross sales - variable costs = gross profit

Gross profit - fixed costs = profit

Key terms here, so I don't overwhelm this chapter with the word "gross."

Gross sales is your top line.

Gross profit is after variable costs.

Profit is gross sales less variable costs less fixed costs.

So when you read "gross" be sure to see if I am referencing gross sales or gross profits.

This is all so key to your business, just want you on the same page as me, because for many of my clients, once they capture this concept, this simple concept, it transforms their business to be more profitable! Let's rock!

Gross profit is taking your gross sales less your variable costs. Variable costs being the costs you really only incur to generate the revenue.

Profit is taking the gross profit explained above less your fixed costs. Fixed costs being the costs you incur no matter what you sell.

The reason I am most interested in gross profit is that is more what determines your profit. How? Profit is first driven by the top number, gross income. If you are not selling enough, you won't have great profits. You can cut expenses all you want, but the biggest factor to profit is gross sales. Make sense? Next, profit is also driven by the variable costs to generate your gross income, that then covers your fixed costs. Make sense? Boom! You got it now.

Stay with me!

These variable costs are easy to lose sight of because of this simple concept. You are spending money now, to generate income later; even if a month later. You pay your labor to build or sell something now, to deliver and collect income next month. You buy products now to sell next quarter. Follow? So you want to ensure when you consider variable costs you are looking at the gross profit of each sale.

What did you sell that service or product for, and what cost did you incur, in addition to your fixed costs, to sell it; and is that direct profit, that gross profit, enough? If you are running a 5% gross profit, when it should be 10%, you have half the gross profit to cover your fixed costs, which is a monumental difference to your bottom line profit. It is easy to think, well, I have to spend this to sell this, so whatever it costs, I gotta have it. Wrong! If you aren't making proper gross profit you need to either raise your price or not sell that service or item. With that being said, this is the easiest area to have waste with your dollars; the variable costs. Lastly, variable costs are typically variable in how much you need at any given time. If you have a seasonal business, you easily will incur more variable costs during a certain part of the year, but again, that will be for future sales, and if you don't properly gauge your future sales, future realistic sales, you will easily incur more variable costs, with them being paid for or incurred ahead of revenue.

Fixed costs, are fixed which leads to less waste because you see the same fixed costs month after month. You know with fixed costs, you are going to have those no matter the revenue which makes it easier to budget and anticipate for. Make sense?

Let me back up to the top line, gross revenue. You really what to look at what's your gross collections, which is the cash basis of accounting. As I discussed in a previous chapter, you can really trick yourself if you are looking only at gross revenue on the accrual basis because that will only reflect what you billed to your clients; not what you collected. It is definitely important to look at what you billed your clients, as that will help you forecast your profit, but your profit to me as a CPA, is what you actually realized. Gross profit and profit on the accrual basis is an anticipation of those actual amounts, yet to be realized.

Many of you may say, I'm not selling widgets so, I'm not buying up inventory and then reselling it. Okay, but most businesses are going to have a direct cost. For example, in a dental practice, the direct cost would be the dentist, hygienist and medical supplies.

Just using that as an example, if you take your gross collections minus your direct cost, that's than your gross profit. If you didn't have any sales, then what would be the expenses that you wouldn't have; is another way to consider variable expenses. What would then be the expenses that you would have no matter what? Meaning, it doesn't matter if you show up to work or not, you are going to have this expense; rent, utilities, phone, insurance, etc. That is your overhead; those are your fixed costs. So the variable cost is inventory but also look at the payroll that would go along with that.

Again, here's why this concept is important. When you are looking at your gross profit, that's actually what's left over to pay your fixed costs. So when you are looking at profit, aka net income, if you are not happy with it, go right to the top line, gross income/revenue.

And if you are happy with the top line, unhappy with your bottom line profit, then look to your variable costs to arrive at a healthier gross profit.

Many businesses start by looking at your fix cost, not saying that you shouldn't, but don't start there. Where you should start is, am I collecting everything that I should? Do I have a high accounts receivable that I'm not collecting?

Am I not selling enough? Am I not charging enough? Then, you can look at it and say, yes, I'm charging and collecting everything I can.

Then you would look at, what is then my variable costs? Am I paying too much for inventory, medical supplies, dental supplies, outsourced services? Not your office supplies or janitorial services; those are fixed costs. Do I have too many direct employees related to generating income? Not your receptionist; that is a fixed cost.

Am I paying too much to my salesforce? Not your bookkeeper; that is a fixed cost. Do I have too many dentists? To many lawyers? Do I have too many hygienists? Are the people that are dedicated to generating revenue standing around? Not because they are lazy or unmotivated, but is there is enough for them to sale, enough for them to do. Do I have too much direct cost/variable cost, because I want to make sure my gross profit is as high as it can be.

Then after asking yourself all those questions, if you say yep, I've done everything I can and I have trimmed there, then you would look at your fixed costs that then effects your profit; your net income.

Here is why it's so key to look at your profit and loss statement in this order.

If you are a small-business owner, that profit, the net income, is what you live on. Am I right? Higher the better. *So last thing I would urge you to look at is, what is the net income before you pay yourself because then you are going to know realistically are you being paid the right amount.*

Business Tips, Secrets

How Long Should I Retain my Files and Records?

JJ THE CPA here. Let's talk about file retention and what is it that you even need to keep around and why.

I have clients all the time that want to know when they can empty out the drawers, when can they get rid of all those documents? With the IRS, if they ever question your tax return, what they're going to want you to prove is that your income recorded on your tax return was correct; whether that's personal or business. So when they're looking at the bank statements, they can see the deposits and where they came from and verify all of that is accounted for as income on the tax return.

When it comes to expenses, especially in a business, they're going to look at whether these are actually business expenses AND if these expenses were paid by the business; or if it's for you, did you pay the expenses that you wrote off.

Here is a little side note, bank statements are not considered documentation for the purposes of substantiating an expense with the IRS. You actually have to have the receipt. The purpose of the bank statement though is to show that the business has paid for it.

Regarding a business, bank statements, credit card statements, receipts, the financials, the general ledger and anything else that goes with the details, you want to retain for six years after the filing date, because that's the statute of limitations that the IRS has to go back and look and request, and sometimes demand, the documents for those years. Same on the individual side. You want to keep anything related to your tax return. I recommend bank statements, savings bank statements, and any other tax documentation such as a Forms 1099, W-2, 1098 (mortgage interest), charitable contributions, etc. that was reflected on your tax return.

So focus in on this. Here's the deal with the IRS, normally if they have a question on your tax return, assuming you are not a drug dealer or something like that, you are going to hear from them within about year from when the tax return was filed, sometimes two years depending on the size of your tax return in terms of the complexity. Normally you are going to know within three years if there's going to be any kind of inquiry from the IRS, but here is how keeping documents comes into play; they may want more than three years back. If you get an audit and they find that you did something, just call it a mistake, say you wrote off something that you didn't know was not a tax-deductible write off; but it is something you did consistently every single year. The IRS can go back and look if you made that same mistake in prior years. But take note of this, they can only go back to 6 years. Also note, if the adjustment is more than 25% of your income, there's a six-year statute that the IRS can look at all of that, whether it's the business or the personal. Assuming there's no fraud, unless the adjustment is more than 25% of your gross income, the statute of limitation is 3 years for the IRS look back at.

So depending on where the years are and the amount of adjustment, that can make a difference on how far they can go back.

The safest thing to do is just keep it 6 years, but then after 6 years you really should just toss it. What would you not toss? If you bought stock and you still own it, you'd want to keep the paperwork showing what your cost basis is. If you bought a home, real estate, or assets even if it's over six years ago you want to keep those documents, because someday you are going to sell it and you will need that documentation to determine the cost basis. So do not think after 6 years you can get rid of any and everything.

Business Tips, Secrets

Does Size Matter? Does the Size of Your Business Matter?

JJ THE CPA here. Let's talk small business owners, about one thing. Know when you have been successful enough.

Many small business owners like myself want to get bigger and bigger. Why? Because they love it, they want to share more of it and they believe they are going to make more money.

From personal experience: I started out just me in 1997. Just me and then I grew. When I hit 10 years, I had 13 people working for me with 6 offices.

Guess what? I was miserable. I wasn't making as much money as I wanted, and what did I do?

I hired more CPAs and I got even bigger; thinking I could delegate my misery away. Then, I decided I got tired of running the business, because when I got into being a business owner of a CPA practice, just like other small business owners, I got into it because I love what I do; helping clients with their taxes. Sound familiar? What happens though, as you grow and grow you no longer are doing what you love to do. All you are doing is running a business and managing people, which then causes you to distance yourself from the customer, your client. Just like I did. So, what did I do? I downsized and got rid of 500 clients and let staff go. On the frontside of this, I bet some of you are thinking, that sounds ridiculous. But guess what, it was a break even for me at first.

In fact, I came out ahead over time because the overhead that I cut and the revenue that I got rid of put me further ahead. How? The revenue given up was less than the expenses I got rid of. This is part of the journey. I now get to enjoy being a CPA again; helping people, and having fun. Heck, it inspired me (and gave me time) to put this book together for you!

So for small business owners out there, as you grow and become for successful, enjoy it. However, if you get to a point where you are taking a shower and you are not looking forward to going into your business because you know it is just going to be one headache after another, that is when you have grown too much and you need to pull it back.

Why do we do what we do? Because we love it. Well, at least I do.

I am adding a P.S. If you are thinking of pulling back by replacing yourself, you can't and you won't. Not possible. So when you pull back, don't just assume you can find a replacement for yourself. Employees aren't owners. And just because you make an employee an owner, they are not an owner like you. They are an employee making more money as an employee because they are getting a piece of the profits because you made them an owner to get compensated more. Making an employee an owner may feel like you are giving them a chance to experience what you experience as a business owner, which is a drive to succeed and manage the business the best as possible. And guess what, you will most likely think you found that one person. And guess what else, at first, they will do all you expect. And then guess what, they get to the point you are at, where they want to pull back, because it's too much and not enjoyable, but guess what else, they can't. They aren't you. You got them to replace you. There is no one to replace them. So what does an employee do. They go get another job. Maybe you are the one in a million that has that one in a billion employee and you are convinced I don't know you or your business, but I know employees. Not only in my own business but with clients who have had employees, and overall I have been involved one way or another with thousands and thousands of employees. And they are never around, not anymore, when you look up 10 years from now. 15. 20. Who will still be there, no matter what. You! So when you decide you need to pull back, look at replacing yourself with 2 or 3 people by breaking up your roles or, make changes to your business.

Remember this. And let this sit with you for a minute. You as a business owner don't make your money based on what you grossed.

You make money based on what you net. So it is possible, no matter what business you are in, to make changes that yes, affect your gross, but not your net. Think on it, because I am looking out for you. Business owner to business owner. Look out for you. No one else is, in your business. And if this statement irritates you... just wait my friend.

MONEY

CASH FLOW

BUSINESS PLAN

PREPARATION

EMOTIONS

LOANS

BANKING

P&L

QUICKBOOKS

UNDERWRITING

NUMBERS

GOAL

FINANCIAL

STATEMENT

Banking secrets

What is the Bank Really Looking at When They are Approving My Loan? Cash is King! But to a Bank, Cash FLOW is King!

JJ THE CPA here. Let's talk about cash flow.

When you are going to get a bank loan, cash flow is king. Not cash on hand. Cash flow. It is the single most important factor for a bank when considering giving you a loan.

Many clients as well as friends think if you are in a situation where you are sitting on $100,000, $500,000 or $750,000 in the bank, and a huge retirement, that you are going to get a loan for $250,000 by walking into the lobby.

Think again! Don't think, this should be a no-brainer for the bank.

Well, unless you are going to put up that money as collateral at the bank, whatever is sitting in your bank account, they're not going to consider that anything other than what you could cover that very day. They may consider it some kind of a soft landing zone if something goes wrong, but you can spend that money tomorrow. Meaning, you could borrow the money and spend the savings that you've got tomorrow, so it means very little to the bank that you've got money in your accounts.

I know you can sit there and think, oh yeah, I have all this money and I am a big time customer. Well, you know what the bank is going to say? Then use your own money, if you have $500,000 sitting there; why are you trying to borrow money? You might reply, you want to use the banks money, right? There's a lot of occasions that it makes sense to use the bank's money to leverage what you are getting into, and the bank wants to loan you money; as that is how they make their bread and butter. But at the same time, having a bunch of cash on hand doesn't make you more suitable for a loan than anybody else. If you have money in retirement, big whippidtydo. You are not able to collateralize it because that money is stuck in there until you are 59 ½.

What they are looking at first is your cash flow. The amount of cash that flows INTO your bank account month after month; and how much they can rely on that cash flow coming in. If you have money sitting around, you can spend it, so why are you coming to us, especially if you have regular cash flow. See where I am going with this?

The bank looks at what you are wanting to do with those dollars, and is it going to generate "more" cash flow. Then, if it's going to generate more cash flow, will it be enough to pay the "new" loan payment to pay off the loan, timely.

Let's walk through this.

- You have put together an idea and now you are going to talk to the bank. In your plan you show that it's going to generate $50,000 a month.

- Are you kidding me bank, why are you not handing me a check right now for my loan request of $500,000?

- I put together an idea that's going to put another $50,000 a month in my account, and by the way I'm going to run it through your bank, so what do you have to worry about?

- First, calm down, you don't get to have any attitude because your idea hasn't generated anything yet. It doesn't generate cash, until it generates cash.

- So if you got something that's going to generate $50,000, great, but what the bank is going to want to look at is what of that $50,000 are you going to net. (Ahhh. Gross profit.)

- If you are doing something related to manufacturing and you are going to bring in $50,000 more a month, but it's contingent on cost of goods sold, what is the percentage of those sales that goes directly to the cost of goods sold or direct sales force?

- That $50,000 might be great but if it costs you 80% in costs ($40,000) to actually generate that $50,000, well, then the bank is looking at situations like... Okay awesome, you generated $50K but you are really only netting $10K before any other expenses.

- Meaning it's going to cost you $40,000 directly to the either the sales rep, the materials or the shipping, so you are only going to net $10,000.

- So all the bank cares about is the $10,000. They are not going to be excited and impressed by that $50,000.

- The other aspect the bank looks at is how much is your overhead is going to be, and how much new overhead is there going to be.

- If you are an existing company and you are expanding, what new overhead will you have? Maybe nothing. You might also be in a situation where it's a brand-new business and it's generating something in addition to what you are doing at a different location.

- Here's my point. What is going to be the additional overhead that you are going to incur to generate these dollars? So if it's just something inside your current offices, or just a new product line where there is no real new overhead just some direct cost, that's one thing, but if you are now opening a second location or it's a brand new business, one of the things at the bank's going to look at is the net profit, after cost of goods sold (variable costs) and additional overhead (fixed costs).

- Okay so you brought in $50,000 and it's going to cost you $40,000 to make that $50,000, but then what's overhead, because that needs to be subtracted. Why? Because again, the bank is looking at cash flow. So if your additional overhead is $1,000 per month, you actual increased cash flow is $9,000 net per month.

- That is what the bank needs to know, and will use to determine if they can loan you money. It's not

$50,000 a month the bank looks at, it would be $9,000 per month. So with an increase of $108,000 in your anticipated additional net profit, the bank will consider that when deciding on your $500,000 loan request.

- You may have been thinking I'm asking to borrow $500,000 with $600,000 of increased gross revenue; so it is no brainer. Right?

Banks loan you money to get paid back and make interest during the time of being paid back. The key for you to fully grasp is, they need to get paid back.

Cash flow is key! Net cash flow. Net increased cash flow from the result of receiving the loan.

Banking Secrets

What Do Banks Look at on My Financial Statements?

JJ THE CPA here. Let's talk about what banks are going to look at when they are looking at your financial statements.

Banks really should be looking at the same things you should be looking at, but the number one priority for the bank is to ensure that you are going to be able to pay them back. In my opinion, they are looking at some key indicators to know what? *Cash flow.* They do not care, typically, how much money you have in the bank compared to how much money you will be putting into the bank. What they will look at is, what are your assets?

The biggest asset the bank is going to look at, typically, is your accounts receivable. What that means is, here is work that you've done but you haven't collected on it. What does that mean to the bank? Cash that should be coming in.

However, here is what they don't like on your accounts receivable (A/R), old aged accounts receivables. Meaning typically most banks if your A/R includes amounts that are older than 90 days, they won't even consider that an asset. They need to assume its non-collectible. What they look at is, what have you done the last 90 days and what are you going to collect on that that. They're going to look at your accounts payable (A/P) as well.

That means that you haven't spent yet but you've received the goods or the services for, so that lets the bank know what else you are having to pay, besides them. If you have a high accounts payable, that's telling the bank you've got a lot of money yet to spend.

What are these relationships to your bank balance? On the financial statements you are looking at your bank balance which is different than what you would see if you logged into your bank, because what's on your financial statement should include any outstanding items, meaning if you wrote a check today and you logged into your bank today your balance will be more accurate on your financial statements because it is going to reflect the check that you just wrote. So, with that, the amount in your bank is going to be more than your financial statements because it just hasn't cleared the bank account.

Why does that matter to a bank?

They can log in to your account and see how much money you have, but that does not give them a true indicator of how much money you have when the checks clear.

Same with deposits and collections. There could be an opportunity when you've collected money but haven't put it in the bank yet, so the bank would be better aware of what your true balance is.

Let's pull it all together. How does the bank balance, A/R and A/P work together from the banks perspective; and yours too, really?

On your financial statements:

Bank balance + accounts receivable − accounts payable = real funds available

Your bank balance, plus your A/R minus your A/P equal the real funds... available to pay anything else... especially... them... the bank.

Banks loan you money to get paid back and make interest during the time of being paid back. Again, the key for you to fully grasp is, they need to get paid back. Funds available is key!

Banking Secrets

Do I Really Need a Business Plan? What is in it?

JJ THE CPA here. Let's talk about the business plan.

Most people only talk about putting together a business plan when they are going to talk the bank about a loan. What is the bank wanting the business plan for? Believe it or not, the first reason they want it, is so they can see that you thought through, your own plan. You can spend a lot of time and effort on a business plan, and you should, but what your defining in a business plan basically is, what is it that you are planning to do? Who are you going to do it for? It is just basically... who, what, where, when, why and how.

When you are doing a business plan, you want to create a summary that includes what your business is going to provide in the such-and-such area to this demographic, at this price with this cost and with this profitability. It does not have to be 10 to 20 pages with a ton of market analysis because the bank is basically going to take your word for it. What they really will be focusing on is your projected financials, not the sales pitch part of the business plan. You should not be in a situation where you would have to prove your data to the bank, because you should have already proved it to yourself. Follow?

When you are putting together the business plan, think of it as if you were trying to prove to yourself that this was a good plan, and what would be the questions asked. I know right off the bat whenever most are getting into a deal as a business owner, many are ready to just jump in.

If we are getting ready to expand, we are ready to go. If it sounds good to us and makes a lot of sense, maybe you have got the opinion of others, your spouse, or friends. The business plan can still be a great idea because it will show you what the plan is from the standpoint of timing, what it will take, and help you focus in. So many times when you are either doing an expansion or starting a new business, you are wearing so many hats, that it can be easy for minor things to slip, not intentionally, but minor things like if you place an ad on Facebook and you let it run and go and let it run for three months, well maybe you should have stopped to look and see if it's yielding any results, so you do not put yourself in a situation to keep paying for something that is not working. Point is when you are putting together a business plan, you are talking about all aspects of what you are getting ready to do, from the perspective of ownership. Then if you put that business plan together, you are going to be in a great position when you are talking to the bank to better know what it is that you are trying to do. Most business owners ask themselves, why am I doing this, to make more money, to expand my business so I can help more people. A business plan puts together that road map. Many business startups or expansions are started too quickly. A business plan allows for more things to be considered with the who, what, where, when, why and how.

Cash flow, the demographic, how to reach those customers, what is the timing, how are you going to market and handle the marketing, and who is going to be one overseeing and managing it all. I know, as a small business owner a lot of that is probably going to be you.

However, what will be the criteria that once you reach a certain level you need to have someone come in and help you?

Do this, go google business plan, it's a simply, who – what – where –why and how. It's just that easy.

So again, don't just think of doing a business plan when you go talk to the bank about a loan. Think about doing it when you are getting into business, or expanding your business; even if the bank doesn't need to see it.

Banking Secrets

What is the Banks Goal When They Loan Me Money?

JJ THE CPA here. Let's talk about the goal of the bank when lending you money.

Most of you think it is because they want to be your friend. I hear it all the time. Seriously, most are thinking, well if I need money, they'd be lucky to get my business. If it's a friend, surely they are going to want a loan money to me, I've been with his bank a long time; I deposit a lot of money there, so they should give me a loan, easy. Here is the thing to know. Yes banks are there to help you, but they make money by loaning you money. It is a business. Not a friendship. And they only survive by getting paid back in full.

Banks are making money off the interest on loans they make from the average daily deposit balances in their bank. So, I want you think about one thing. If you are like most small businesses, you can deposit 1.2 million dollars per year in a bank, but what's your average daily balance? It is probably not 1.2 million dollars. You would be an exceptional business if you had $50,000 in your business account at any one time. Therefore, that bank only really has access to your average daily balance when it comes to deposits on hand to make loans easily to you.

Banks can use all of the customers reserves to loan money out. Therefore, if they are loaning you more money than your average daily balance, they are loaning you money from another customers reserves.

Follow? And, with that being said, the banks are going to want to make sure that you are going to pay them back. Because that is the bank's goal, to get paid back.

It takes a good relationship with the bank, they need to trust you and if you have been in business for a while, they are going to want to see that you are depositing a lot of funds, regularly. They want to see that cash flow is reliable. My point is, many think that because they deposit 1.2 million dollars in their bank, the bank is lucky to have their business. All that thinking does is put you in a situation where you think that you are going to be able to just get a million-dollar loan because you run a million plus dollars through their bank. What I want you to think through is, this bank needs to know that they're going to get their money back, as that's their goal, and it's not because you say so, it's not because you think you have the best idea ever and it's not because you are in a situation where your friends with them either. It is because you've got an idea that is going to generate cash flow that will then service that loan. It is not about how much money you have sitting there, it's about cash flow and how it will service that loan. Because, again, the bank's goal is to get paid back; just the same as if you are the one loaning money to someone else.

Banking Secrets

How Do I Put Myself in the Best Position to Get a Loan?

JJ THE CPA here. Let's talk about how to put yourself in the best position for a loan. What is the secret? Be fully prepared when you ask for a loan, including having your documents already ready to share.

If you are prepared and ready to give the bank whatever it needs and wants, before they ask, or immediately after asking, you are putting yourself in the best position because it shows the bank you know your numbers and they can work through the process easier, quicker and without much delay. Probably more than that, be able to provide bank with what you need, why you need it, how you will use it and how it will generate more revenue. The bank doesn't want to loan the max they can lend you. They want to loan you what you need. And your need is defined by why you need it and how it translates to more money coming in the door. This is the process the banks will go through with you, so if you can go through most of that before you talk to your banker, that puts you in the best position as you will be prepared.

Let's talk about financial statements and what it is that you are wanting to pull together for the bank. First thing is they're going to want to see three years' worth of financial statements, and usually those are going to be the three most recent complete years, plus then year-to-date financials. You want to make sure that those financials are going to match the tax return, because the first thing for you to know is that the bank is going to take your financials and compare them to your tax returns. Why? Simply because if you file something with the IRS then it is filed under penalties of perjury that it's correct, and the bank is going to probably rely on that. But banks will not just want your tax returns as they're going to want to see your financials. Here is why... they are double-checking the information you are giving them. By doing so, they have it from two sources. I have personally gone around and around with banks before because I say, these are the tax returns and the financials are no different. But the bank still wants to see the financials. You know why else, because the regulators want to see it, so the bank underwriters are going to ask for that. If you can have financial statements ready to rock, because you know they're going to ask for the tax returns, then you are going to be already that much further head. But here's the thing, don't just whip out financial statements and send them to the bank. Again, you want those financial statements to already match the tax return. So if you hand in financials to your bank and you didn't run it by your CPA or even double-check yourself that they match the tax returns, you just put yourself behind the eight ball because the underwriter is potentially going to say none of this matches, so how do I know what's right. You need to be in a situation where they match, so the underwriter is not going to be questioning what it is that you've put together. I don't mean questioning this must be fraudulent; they are going to just question why it doesn't match. Guess what you've done? You just delayed the process of getting the loan done. You have drawn them to ask more questions which then requires more documents.

How do you know that your tax returns and your financials match?

- Depending on the tax return that you are filing whether it's a Form 1120, 1120S or 1065 all of them are going to have what's called a schedule L. It's a full page you can't miss it. It's either page four or five of your business tax return (depending on which).

- When you look at that it's going have two main columns on Schedule L, one is the balance sheet as of the prior year. Example, if you were looking at a tax return for year 2020 on that schedule L you would see a major column that says as of 12/31/19 and you would see a column that says as of 12/31/20.

- When you are looking at your 2020 financials you then would want to look at the column that is 12/31/20 and then you look at your balance sheet. Sometimes that is called a statement of assets and liabilities. How do you even know what it is that you are looking at? The way that you know, is on that financial statement it's going to indicate assets at the top, cash, bank account, etc.

- If you look at your financials it will indicate what your *total assets* are, so when you are looking at your *total assets* on that schedule L, on your tax return, you are going to see a line item that says *total assets* and they should match.

- What if they don't match? It's not panic time. It does not mean the financials are wrong, it doesn't mean the tax returns are wrong. What it means is most likely something was put on the tax return and that adjustment just didn't get made to your financials. What is that typically? It's typically depreciation. So do not panic, because now you know without the bank having to tell you, that your financials don't match the tax return. Now you can say, okay well I just need to figure that out and I need to talk to my CPA. So know this before providing it to the bank; the reason why there is a difference.

- So now when you are looking at your *total liabilities* and equity, on the same financial statement that you are looking at, you'll see another major total that will say *total liabilities*. When you look on that schedule L on your tax return there's going to be a line item that says that as well, so you are just comparing.

- Now most likely and I'd say 100% of the time, if you are in a situation where your assets do not match the financials and the tax return, well then your assets not matching means your liabilities are not going to match because this is a balance sheet and those things need to balance. Still you need to take a look just to make sure, many times if it doesn't match what it can be is that the balances on your loans at year end just were not updated for the amount of interest that was paid in the prior-year.

- These are just two common situations where it's easy for the financials to not get updated right at the year-end, but it's not uncommon for depreciation to not have been recorded on the financials or any kind of adjustment for interest. There is also a couple other things that might just be easy to pop out but wouldn't you rather be the one that goes, oh these don't match and it's not time to panic, it's not time to wake up your CPA in the middle of the night and accuse them of not doing their job or doing things wrong, because those are *your* books, those are *your* financials, it's *shared* problem if they don't match. You should then say hey CPA you know what the tax return and the financials do not match up, so can you look? Usually, at least in our office, we already know what those differences are, it may just be that we hadn't been out to your office yet to make the adjustment.

By doing all of this, see how you have reduced down a lot of questions and headache by just taking a minute and matching them up and making sure that they do, and if they don't, then trying to solve that problem before you go to the banker.

Major thing, we answer so many questions from the banks and I'll bet you 50% of them are in these circumstances where the financials didn't match the tax return; with easy explanations. It was no one's fault, it was just simply an adjustment that had not been made due to timing.

Either way, it's all solvable.

Would you not rather solve it before you get to the bank? The answer is yes.

So to put yourself in the best position for a loan, be fully prepared when you ask for the loan, including looking over your documents and having them ready to share.

Banking Secrets

What Do I Need To Be Ready To Discuss With My Bank When I Get a Loan?

JJ THE CPA here. So you are ready to talk to the bank? You got your documents ready! Now, let's discuss what you need to do to be ready for that talk.

Before you even approach a bank, do you know what you need to know? First, you must know your numbers and you need to have your financial statements in play here. Meaning, you need to know the numbers on the documents you are giving them. Easy! They are expecting you to walk in and know what it is that you need the money for, where it's going to go, and what ideas that you've come up with on how they're going to get paid back.

Why? Because it is based on cash flow.

You are going to want to have your financials to share, but look at them before the meeting. Look at the things we discussed before. They are major line items, and easy to spot, but look at them before you talk with your banker, and be familiar with the numbers. It's okay to pull the financials out, and give them a copy. But don't be fumbling to find the numbers. Know where they are. These...

- Gross revenue.

- Variable Costs (Costs of Goods Sold).

- Gross Profit.

- Fixed Expenses (Overhead).

- Profit.

- Your compensation.

- You A/R.

- Your A/P

Now, if you are an existing business, you'll have these historically. Be familiar with last year's numbers and the year-to-date numbers as well. If you are not an existing business, you need to be in a situation where you can have some financials that will depict what is going to happen; with the above numbers laid out.

Remember this, you are not selling yourself, in terms of the product or service that you are selling, you are selling your company in terms of cash flow.

You want to be in a situation where you can show that you are going to pay back this loan out of the cash flow. So be confident and know your numbers. Know what you are doing, why you are doing it and think of it this way, if someone was coming to ask you for money what would you want to know? The secret is just being prepared and knowing what it is that you want, how to get it, and making sure you are asking for the right amount of loan, so that you share with the bank how you will have the cash flow to meet their primary goal, which is to be paid back.

Your numbers is what you need to be ready to discuss with the bank!

Banking Secrets

That Bank is Lucky to Have My Business, So Why is it so Emotional When I Get a Loan?

JJ THE CPA here. Let's talk about not getting emotional about getting a loan.

So, stop getting emotional about it. Like, right now.

This is not an emotional decision for the bank. I get it, its emotional for you; but what you need to understand is as I have discussed in other chapters, the banks just want to make sure they will get paid back, that's all.

Yes, they got questions and you just need to be prepared to answer them. And you cannot get all mad about it because basically, when you start getting upset what do you think the banks is going to think about that? The bank is going to wonder why you are so frustrated that they are asking some questions? Questions do not mean that they are not going to give you the loan, but you don't want to be in a circumstance where someone is wondering why you are being a jerk. Just think if you had a customer and you call him and say, hey we are ready to come out and do the service, and they are a total jerk about it and start asking you, why is it taking so long, when are you going to be done, etc. What is your reaction going to be? Be honest. You are probably going to be hesitated to ever do business with them again.

To make sure the bank is going to get paid back, all the bank can do is ask questions, right? They aren't in your business. The bank does not have an office in yours. So be patient. Be polite. If they aren't asking questions, it may not be a good sign. And if they haven't said no, keep answering their questions.

It's emotional because you are worried you are going to be turned down for the loan, which means you will have been rejected. No one wants to be rejected, business reasons or not. That is why it is so emotional to the person asking for the loan. And the thought if they don't get the loan. However, it's a 50/50 inquiry. Yes or no. They will either loan it or they won't. Your emotions, don't increase your chances, but could hurt your chances.

Banking Secrets

What Should I Memorize for The Sit With My Bank?

JJ THE CPA here. Let's talk about what to memorize during the sit down with the bank. There are many things to be prepared for, as we talked about in previous chapters. However, here is what you need to memorize:

What did you gross last year?

What were your costs last year?

What did you net last year, before you paid yourself?

They will also want the same numbers for the current year, but you will need to find out from what period, you cannot just say year to date. If you have financials through June 30th and you are talking to the bank in August, you would want to make them aware this is through June 30th. These are numbers you will just want to know and can spit out. Do not fumble around through paperwork to answer those questions as these are the most basics numbers, and you need to just know them.

And guess what, by memorizing them, you will know them for your purposes. You aren't really memorizing these numbers for the bank. It's not to impress them, or trick them into thinking you know your numbers. If you memorize the numbers, you WILL know them. Follow?

They may ask you how much money you have in the bank, even if you bank with them, they may still ask this. Do not answer this question, as of today? Yes, that is why they are asking that question, as of today how much money do you have in the bank.

They will also want to know how many assets you have in the business; just round it. It is on your balance sheet and if you are not sure ask your CPA.

The bank is also going to want to know total liabilities and they will want to know how much money you have put in the business. I know that might sound like a lot, but it's not, you can have a cheat sheet in front of you with all these numbers on it. And guess what your cheat sheet is? Your financials. And oh, they have a copy too! So don't get all nervous. Pull them out. Look at them. Know them, but use your financials as your guide. Be comfortable with your financials. Follow?

Do not be nervous, they just want to know totals. By being able to tell them all these numbers you are helping them determine one thing, cash flow; which has been discussed a lot in this book. If you can get these numbers memorized. Then you will literally be 1 in a 100 of small business owners who sit down with a bank and 1 in 1,000 who know their numbers.

Know your numbers, know your business.

If you don't know your numbers, you don't know your business.

Banking Secrets

How Much of a Line of Credit Do I Need?

JJ THE CPA here. Let's talk about how much of a line of credit you need.

It comes down to three months. Three months of overhead expenses is what your line of credit should be, even on the personal side.

So, if your overhead is $10,000 a month for your house payment, car payment and to keep the household running, then a $30,000 personal line of credit is what you need. For a business, say your overhead is $50,000 a month to pay employees and keep the lights on, you should want a line of credit of $150,000.

Does either one of these sound like you? Take what your overhead is and multiple that by 3, that will be what your line of credit should be to keep things going.

It is just that simple.

Banking Secrets

What Do I Do When I Have a Financial Crisis?

JJ THE CPA here. Let's talk about when you have hit a financial crisis and need to talk to the bank? Stop. Don't talk to them first.

If you are in a situation like this, here is what the bank does not want to hear, that you are in financial crisis. Don't overreact and do not go to your bank in a panic. This isn't to hide anything from your bank, but here is the thing, the bank does not necessarily see it as a crisis, the bank may not be in a panic.

If you are in a situation where you have done that, did you first talk to your CPA? No.

Then go talk with them so that you can figure things out and better assess what the issues are, really.

Second thing to look at is, what are the legal issues that you are dealing because here is what the bankers want to hear, are you ready for this? They want to hear one thing, what are you going to do about it? So, when you walk in and you say, I have a situation and my partner left or are major vendor is no longer is in business, so we must find another vendor and they are more expensive. Whatever the problem is, if they know that you've already defined it, know how long is it going to last and what are you going to do about it, you will be much better off.

Remember we talked about removing emotions when dealing with your bank, because it is not emotional for them? The same applies here.

Get with your team of professionals to see if you are in a financial crisis, for real, and come up with a game plan, to then approach the bank with. So in no way am I advocating to keep things from your bank that have a major financial crisis wrapped around it. They need to know, but properly.

Remember this, a bank is not interested in loaning you money if you do not know how you are going to pay them back, you do not know your cash flow and you do not know your way out of it. The banks role, typically, is not to develop a plan with you to get out of whatever you are in, when looking at overhead, wages, your direct costs and your gross revenue. They might be able to help you figure out how to get out of it from a cash flow standpoint, but you would need to know all those things up front. You need to have a plan and be able to tell the bank what you are going to do, tell them you talked to your CPA and here are my last two years of the financials, and I have put together a quick forecast of things that I see that I'm going to change.

Financial crisis? That is why you want an existing team of trusted professionals available to you.

Banking Secrets

How Can I Help My Credit Ratings?

JJ THE CPA here. Let's talk about credit ratings, as it relates to whether you are carrying debt or your debt-free.

Here is what's odd, and you are going to probably going to question this, but if you are debt-free it does not help your credit rating. What helps your credit rating is having debt and then being able to show that you can handle the debt and make regular payments. With my daughter, who is now out on her own, I wanted her to get a credit card and start building up some credit. I told her when you get a credit card you are going to need to charge some things on it. First just get stuff that you need, but then you need to carry a balance. So, if you charge a couple hundred dollars and you pay it off the next month, you've done nothing to help your credit. I know that sounds weird, but what you want to do is charge up a couple hundred dollars, and then make more than the minimum payment. This helps your credit the most. Carrying balances and paying on time.

Banking Secrets

Should I Get a Home Equity Loan? I Can Then Tax Deduct the Interest, Right?

JJ THE CPA here. There is a new provision in the tax law that is not favorable, and it has to do with home equity loans. It used to be with home equity loans, you got a tax deduction for the interest expense as long as the amount of your loan, regardless if it was a first, second, or third, did not exceed the original cost of the home. However, under the new tax law, if you have a loan for anything other than your home, the interest is not tax deductible. So, if you got a second mortgage to help pay for college tuition, or any personal expenses, you are not going to get that tax deduction.

VEHICLE

CPA

REFUND

LIKE KIND EXCHANGE

SECRETS

ACCOUNTANT

IRS

TAXES

PLANNING

CREDIT CARD

DECOR

GIFTS

INCOME EA

MONEY

STRATEGY

DEDUCTIONS

Tax Strategies

Do I Really Need a CPA or Enrolled Agent (EA)? Yes!

JJ THE CPA here. Let's talk about why it is important that you hire a CPA or an EA to do your taxes.

If you already have one, you are awesome, smart and extremely good looking! Might just skip this chapter!

Both of these professionals have taken the time to go above and beyond to learn what it is that they are doing to be able to prepare tax returns properly. I always joke... when you go get a haircut do you still go to your mom; if you don't, why is she still doing your tax return? Here's the other thing, if you have plumbing issues, normally you do not hire your neighbor. If you need to have some stitches put in, do you just run across the street, knock on your neighbor's door and ask if anybody can stitch you up? I doubt it. If you have a cavity, do you call your dad and ask him to bring the drill over and fix the cavity? I am going to assume the answer is no. Why is it that you are hiring somebody to do those other things, and then not hiring a CPA or EA? Why is it that when it comes to your taxes, you are doing them yourself or using someone that is not qualified?

What is an Enrolled Agent, an EA? An EA is somebody that is enrolled with the Internal Revenue Service and that the IRS has deemed as qualified to prepare tax returns. Doesn't necessarily mean they are experienced or have expertise in all things taxes; just the same with a CPA. However, better than a neighbor, friend, co-worker or family member preparing your tax returns, an Enrolled

Agent has taken an exam that is administered and created by the Internal Revenue Service and they've passed it to get those credentials; EA. They are required to get annual continuing education on tax issues, and is somebody that can represent you before the IRS; which is huge.

With a CPA, it is the same in that we have to pass the CPA exam, be approved by the IRS and get continuing education. Now the CPA, in my opinion, is a step above the EA. Here's why, on the CPA side it is full encompassing related to accounting, bookkeeping, financials, audit, governmental accounting, tax, business law, etc. With an Enrolled Agent it is just the tax.

If you are having tax returns done, you need to make sure the person is an EA or a CPA so that way you know that they are qualified to do your tax return.

What blows me away, is that everyone is so afraid of the IRS, but when it comes to their tax return they will use someone that is not qualified or cheap. If you have any concerns about the IRS, why would you worry about if something's going to cost you $200 or $1,200 to prepare an individual return or more with a business return, when it is the most important thing you file every year, with the Federal government no less. Make sure you are dealing with somebody that is trained in what they're doing. You do it with everything else, so do it with your taxes.

Tax Strategies

What Should I Be Doing At the Beginning of the Year for Taxes?

JJ THE CPA here. We're going to talk about what to do at the first of the year.

First thing is we start planning for the year we are in. Last year is over. Put it to bed. Close out the prior year books and get tax returns done asap.

Next, we look at how the prior year looked and if the upcoming year will be different. Why? Because that will be your first indicator on how the taxes will be different for the year you are in. So to be sure we are on the same page, if you are in year 2020, as in present and physically in January 2020, you would close out 2019 and be looking ahead to 2020.

One of the first things to look at is, from a tax perspective, did you have any large purchases in the prior year because if you did you then you probably had a massive amount of depreciation in the prior year that you will not have in the year you are in, unless you buy another round of assets in a similar amount. That will be your first clue and difference on what it is between the prior year and the current year.

Do the same exercise with any out of the norm expenses and income. Maybe you had a huge month that won't happen in the current year or you had a huge expense other than assets in the prior year, you won't have in the current year. Those differences are your starting point of how the current year will be different.

Next, look at what will be different this year with special purchases, expenses or revenue. Maybe last year you didn't buy assets but you plan to this year. Maybe in the prior year you didn't have any huge months, but you know an upcoming month will have extraordinary income because of a huge job you are wrapping up. Those differences come into play, just the same.

So with that information, look at what was the taxable income of the prior year and adjust for the things different in the current year to arrive at an initial estimate of taxable income for the current year.

Let's run a quick example: If you bought $100,000 worth of assets in the prior year, that saved you 35% on Federal taxes, and in my home state also another 5% on Oklahoma taxes. So, you are talking about a 40% tax savings or $40,000. So, if everything is equal with everything else in the current year in terms of income and expenses, but you don't have that $100,000 deduction in the current year, you should know right now your taxes are going to be $40,000 more than last year. There is no reason to get mad at your CPA or EA. It's not anybody's fault, but at the first of the year you should be prepared for that, because if you have another $40,000 due taxes if you started saving for it right now, you have 52 weeks, and that is less than a thousand a week that you need to be setting aside.

Another thing you want to look at when you are at the beginning of the year is what are the due dates in the current, upcoming year. Meaning what are you coming upon. This why you want a CPA/EA; to help you remember.

Based on when this book was written, the first thing you need to know is that by January 31st you need to be sending Form 1099s to anybody that you paid over $600 to in the prior year. There are some rules around that, but basically if your business has paid an individual over $600 then you have to send that person a Form 1099. If they provided a service to you, even if they are a business, you will most likely need to send them a Form 1099 as well. Just giving the basics, and the obvious. Check with your CPA/EA.

If you are in a situation where you have employees, hopefully you are using a payroll company, but if you are doing your own payroll, by January 31st you've got to file Form 940, Form 941 and you have to make sure that all the taxes have been paid in for the prior year.

Typically for your state you are going to have some kind of year-end reports due as well. You need to get your Form W-2s to the employees by the end of January, and you need to get your Form W-3 with your W-2s to the IRS basically by the end of January. I know there are all kinds of exceptions to some of these things, and depending on if your non-profit or if you file online, these are just the general deadlines.

But then on your business return, depending on how you are taxed, you have due dates coming with that. On your individual tax returns you have quarterly estimated tax payments coming due. Again, get with your CPA/EA for actual due dates.

That seems like a lot, but it's not. What I would do is sit down with the calendar and put those due dates on it a the beginning of the year with reminders two weeks from the due date, set to recur annually.

Now that we are in the new year we shouldn't be doing much to wrap up the prior year other than matching December to the bank statement, get those financials closed and giving that to the CPA, so that they can get the tax return done. If you find yourself in January saying what did last year look like, meaning that's the first time you are looking at last year's numbers and you are just now entering in bank statements and reconciling 12 months. Then use this time to go ahead and get that done for prior year. But then right now in the first of the year don't think you have exhausted yourself to the extent that you think that since you got everything done for the prior year, you will get started on the current year next January, a year later. Do not do that. Get started on the current year

right now.

The point of the chapter is that I want you to be in a the

situation where you are looking ahead, and thinking what

it is that you can do now to be prepared for what is ahead.

So at the first year, get prepared for the entire year ahead.

Tax Strategies

JJ, What Secret Deductions Are There in Tax Season?

JJ THE CPA here. Let's talk about the secrets during tax season.

I had several clients ask me this over the years and so I thought, why not pass along those secrets to you! They ask, JJ what else can I do to knock my numbers down? Any secrets? My response, every time. Phew... not much. Once the year is over it's over. Meaning once prior is over there are not very many ways that you can save any additional taxes for the prior year, other than putting money into an HSA or an IRA; which you have until April 15th. If you are in a state that you can deduct 529 plans, typically you can deduct on your prior year tax return, the contributions you make on or before April 15th, but only at the state level. However, we are not talking much there and those things are limited. If you are self-employed, you can put money into a SEP plan, and you have until the due date of the tax return, including extensions to fund and get the deduction for the prior year. Those are good deductions because you are giving those funds to yourself. Meaning you are putting money into retirement, education and medical for you and your family. However, the bottom line is, in terms of additional expenses or anything to that effect, you are not able to do much about your prior year taxes, once the year ends.

So, here is the secret during tax season, if your CPA is good at giving you the results, figure out what the differences between the prior year and the current/upcoming year. What is the current/upcoming year going to look like? What I mean by that is what was the prior year's income and is it going to be like that in the current/upcoming year. If you own a small business, are you expecting the same, if so, what are some things that you now until the end of the upcoming year to save yourself some taxes? I know, it sounds bleak, but it's not, and that is the real secret. That is the secret sauce, start planning now.

So the secret to tax season is to determine the current year estimated tax so you can determine now what to do, to save tax in the current year, so next tax season is what you are prepared for. Make sense?

Tax Strategies

Why Don't You Like Refund Anticipation Loans JJ?

JJ THE CPA here. Let's talk about a way to ensure you keep all of your tax refund.

This is important. Do not get anticipation tax refund loan. Just do not do it.

When you go to get your tax returns prepared, if you are offered a tax refund anticipation loan just say, no thanks. Yes, it might feel good that you are going to walk out that day with cold hard cash on a card you can swipe and run to the mall immediately, but don't do it. Why? Check this out, on the Form 1040 there is section where you simply put your banking routing and account numbers, answer if it is a checking or savings account and then the IRS has literally a high priority to get you your money back ASAP.

In today's world, if you cannot get a checking account there are plenty of options available to you. You can go into Wal-Mart, Walgreens, Target, etc. and get a debit card that is loadable. Make sure you get a card that can receive a direct deposit. You can get that account set up while in your car. Then you will get your money within about 5 to 10 business days on average. Sometimes much quicker than that. By doing that, not only do you have your money pretty quick, you did not pay a huge fee.

That is why you don't want to get a refund anticipation loan, because you are going to pay a high fee that could be from $100 - $400 (or more). So skip the loan and get your refund direct deposited, save fees and keep more of your money.

Tax Strategies

What Are the Sexy Business Vehicle Deductions?

JJ THE CPA here. Let's talk about business vehicle deductions.

If you have a vehicle that you are using for your business, any expenses that you incur as it relates to that vehicle, you can write off.

There is one caveat, when you are making the payment for the purchase of a vehicle, the payment is not something that you are able to tax deduct because when you bought the vehicle with a business loan that is when you took the deduction. The part of your loan payment that is deductible, is the interest.

So when you are getting near year-end and you are thinking through what you can do to get some tax deductions, prepaying or making a large payment towards your car loan is not going to do it.

If you lease a vehicle through your business, that can be a good idea under certain circumstances, for those that are not driving lots of miles and if you want a new car every 3 years or so. When you are leasing a vehicle, the payment is considered rent. So when you make a payment on your lease that is when you get the deduction, not upfront when you sign the lease the vehicle. If your business is an S-Corp, Partnership, sole proprietorship and you have a vehicle in your business, you are going to be a cash basis taxpayer.

Why does that matter?

When you are cash basis you can pay up to 12 months in advance on any expenses, even though they're prepaid and deduct in the year you pay it. So, if by 12/31 you pay the next 12 payments on your vehicle lease you are in a situation where you are going to be able to deduct all those payments.

If you are paying, regardless if the vehicle is leased or owned, the car washes, gasoline and any kind of repairs you get to deduct. Make sure the insurance on the car is being paid out of your business, so you can deduct that as well.

With any business vehicle the key there and what the IRS looks at in the event of audit, first and foremost, is the business on the title.

Secondly, they are going to look at, financed or leased, is the business on the loan or lease, because those two things make it then a business tax deduction, to the extent of business use.

It can't just be that you pay the vehicle expenses through the business. It needs to be that the business was on the title and the financing was through the business. Sometimes with that, you can get into a circumstance where you are being told by the car dealership that if the business is going to finance the vehicle that it will be a higher interest rate. Know this, you can lease or finance the vehicle personally, as well as through the business, if you just have your business guarantee it. Then when you go to title it, you can have your name on the title as well as the business. The key is the business must be involved in both, and then make sure you are paying everything that you can before 12/31. Again, paying the principal loan doesn't count but paying the lease does.

What if you do not have a business vehicle, but you are using a car for business? Then you can deduct mileage, and by deducting that you now get to pay yourself a mileage rate for each mile that you are driving for your business. Each year the IRS changes the rate and it will also depend on what part of the year those miles were driven. So you want to get with your CPA to figure out what the mileage rate is for the time that you incurred those miles, and make sure that you are writing yourself an expense reimbursement check before year end so you get the tax deduction. Without having the business reimburse you for the business miles, you won't realize the tax deduction.

Tax Strategies

I Am Giving Some Money to a Family Member, So Can I Get a Charitable Tax Deduction Please? Nope.

JJ THE CPA here. Let's talk about when you are giving gifts to family.

Here is what I want you to know, it is not deductible, and it is not charitable to give money or anything else to a family member, and here is why. Pretty much the only thing that you get to deduct in this manner is giving to a 501(c)(3) that is a tax-exempt charitable organization that will give you a receipt, especially if you have given $250 or more. When you are giving to a couple bucks to the person on the street or you are giving to your family, it is not deductible. If you give $25 to a teacher, that is not deductible. However, if you give something directly to a school, get a letter from them to indicate what they received (if over $250), because there is a way to deduct what you donate to your children's school.

If you are giving to a university, you need to make sure that it's done through an organization that is typically their Foundation, which is the charitable arm of the University.

Be mindful that just because you give out of the kindness of you heart, that does not necessarily lead to a tax deduction because it must be to a qualifying entity.

Here is a little secret to share. When you are giving to a charitable organization, it will need to state on the receipt that "no goods or services were provided," and if there were any goods or services provided, the organization will send you a receipt saying that you received X amount in good or services, and this net amount is deductible. So if you have to a charitable event, but received a t-shirt, the cost of the t-shirt must be subtracted from the amount you gave.

For sure, get a receipt!

Tax Strategies

I Need to Trade In My Business Vehicle to Avoid Tax, Right?

JJ THE CPA here. Let's discuss the new law when it comes to like kind exchanges. Trading one business asset for another; trading in a vehicle.

Under the new law here is the big thing, it is only now allowed on real property, as in real estate.

No longer are you allowed to trade in your vehicle, and it be a tax-free transaction. You can trade in your car all day long but in terms of it being a like kind exchange that would kick the can on the tax implications, is no longer available.

The law basically says on tangible assets there is no longer available the like kind exchange. Now there is an expiration on that, but between now and then, if you are in a circumstance where you traded in a vehicle or machinery, you could be in a situation to where that event (the trade), is now taxable because you did a like kind exchange. What does that mean? You traded in one asset for a similar asset. This means you are going to need to do some planning with your CPA because that will lead to a tax hit when you get rid of a business vehicle or asset. Why? Because if you have traded in a vehicle or asset a number of times in the past, for your business, you will now need to recapture, under normal circumstances all of the prior year gains that were then deferred and included in the new basis of the new vehicle. So, what does all that mean? You are staring down a big taxable gain, with tax right behind it.

How do you combat this? If needed, replace the asset sold, in the same year you sold it. Buy another, similar vehicle, in the year you traded the prior vehicle. What does this accomplish? You are picking up a tax deduction on the new purchase that can offset, indirectly, the taxable gain on the sale or trade. Why in the same year? Because you can only tax deduct any expense in the year of purchase, and so if you don't purchase in the same year as your sale or trade, you will be experiencing one year with taxable gain, with no offset to that tax, and the next year with a tax deduction, unable to offset. Not one size fits all, but you get the drift!

If you are buying and selling personal vehicles, this does not apply to you because you never wrote the vehicle off to begin with.

It is very rare, but if you do sell a car for more than you paid for it, even if personally, you do need to pay tax on that gain.

Tax Strategies

Can I Deduct That? Can I Deduct This? What? I Can? How?

JJ THE CPA here. Let's talk about how anything has the possibility of being tax deductible.

Is buying flowers tax deductible? If you immediately say no, then you are missing the boat because under Internal Revenue Code (IRC) section 162 it does not state that flowers are or are not tax deductible. What you will find under IRC section 162 is that if an expense is ordinary or necessary for your business and your intent is for business purposes, then you can tax deduct it.

I have clients that either have an unfortunate situation come up or even a celebratory situation that happens, and I send them flowers. I will write those off, because my intent is for business. The interesting angle here is, some may say that is fishy because I am writing that off, but it is an ordinary expense, and my intent is for business, so I have met the qualifications to tax deduct the flowers I bought. If you are sending flowers to a loved one on your anniversary, then of course you cannot write that off.

Now apply this to anything.

Is a motorcycle a tax deduction? Yes, if used for business. Yes, if owned by a security company that uses motorcycles in protecting its clients.

Are pink ballet shoes tax deductible?

Yes, if you own a ballet studio. Yes, if you are a professional dancer.

It does come down to ordinary to your business. Those things above are considered ordinary to the business mentioned. Those items were bought with intent to use for business purposes. Those items are then tax deductible.

Tax Strategies

Tax Season is Over, Now What?

JJ THE CPA here. Let's talk about what to do when tax season is over.

What are you going to do now? Start or continue planning for the year you are in, right now for your taxes due next April. Know what you paid in last year, so you can be sure to pay the same this year, assuming all things being equal, and you didn't owe a ton or have a huge refund; as you would want to adjust accordingly to avoid either.

Here are the steps. Get your tax return out. Your personal tax return, Form 1040. Now the Form changes each year, so I am not going to list specific line number, but I know you can read, so find the lines on your Form 1040 that say the words below.

1. Go to the line item that says **total tax**.

2. Find out what you paid in federal withholdings and estimated tax payments. That is what you paid in. You will see a line item that says **total payments**.

3. Take your tax and compare that to your total payments. You now see why you got a refund or you owed. Simple enough. Most don't know this; and how that is determined. Total tax less total payments equals refund/owe.

4. If refund or amount owed are numbers that are significant to you, then you need to adjust what you are paying in or having withheld.

5. It's that simple. Now you are planning.

Why is this important to you? Because you do not want to get to next April and have the same results. If it's a significant refund, that is not smart, because even though we love our government, why give them a loan all year. If you are getting a $1,200 - $12,000 refund back, it might feel good in the moment, but that is another $100 - $1,000 a month you could be putting in your pocket to do other things with.

Now if you owe big time, I bet it felt like a wallop. So, act. Start setting money aside or withholding and paying in more with your estimated tax payments. Doing this, you are already on your way to planning. That is the plan, planning for taxes. Next you want to get into strategizing, but again, before you can strategize you have to know where you are at. You must know what your tax is going to be, what are your withholdings, what are you paying in, are you going to owe, or are you getting a refund. You must know those things first, to then strategize.

As you can see it is not hard to figure out. So no more excuses to not knowing.

Tax Strategies

What Are The First Steps to Year-End Tax Planning?

JJ THE CPA here. Let's talk about year-end tax planning and getting prepared for year-end cash flow.

The biggest thing you need to look at when you sit down and think what is my tax for the year; what is it I'm going to have to pay in January and/or April, depending on quarterly estimates or paying it when you get to tax time. You need to know this, so you have those funds ready and available when the time comes.

Then, you look at, what can you do about it. What can you do, before year-end, to reduce those taxes? So you must determine what kind of cash are you going to have available to even be doing any year-end planning because you may want to do $100,000 worth of tax planning but what if you don't have that available? Yes, $100,000 would save you approximately $40,000 in tax, but if you do not have that available, then what?

We are just talking round numbers, so there is no reason to stress yourself out trying to get down to the penny when you are doing your own calculation, because some of the stuff is crystal ball.

Let's run an example:

- So, let's say you have $10,000 in the bank.
- Then give it your best guess on how much do you think you are going to collect between now and the end of the year. Let's just say its $20,000.

- Let's say you also have a line of credit, and on that line of credit you have $30,000 available.

- And you have $10,000 available to spend on your credit card.

- So with $10,000 in the bank, $20,000 more in collections and $30,000 available on your line of credit and $10,000 available on your credit care, you have available $70,000 to work with.

- No, I am not saying you are going to run out and do $70,000 worth of year-end tax-planning. What I am saying is you have $70,000 maximum to work with. You couldn't do $100,000 of tax planning unless you wanted to, in this example. Follow?

- You need to figure out what you *need* to pay between now and the end of the year for payroll, rent and all the basics.

- So, let's say payroll, not necessarily including yourself is $10,000.

- Let's say you have another $20,000 in rent and all the other normal expenses to pay for before year-end.

- So now you have $40,000 to work with. $70,000 available less expected normal expenses of $30,000 nets you $40,000 for year-end planning possibilities.

- Wait, what do you need to pay in January for business expenses?

- Maybe you could prepay a month of rent, utilities, and overhead, that is another $15,000.

- If you did $15,000 in pre-payments, that may save you an estimated $5,000 in taxes coming up on your tax return. I usually round these type of deductions saving about 1/3rd the amount on tax

- Now, whatever you were planning to pay with your next tax estimate in January or the remainder tax in April, will be less by approximately $5,000.

So what is key to year-end tax planning is to first determine what your tax is, so you know what you could save with any year-end tax planning. Next, you need to know how much you have available to do any year-end tax planning with. With all that, you can determine what the year-end tax planning will save you, which is the whole point.

Tax Strategies

When is End of the Year Tax Planning Being Done?

JJ THE CPA here. Let's talk about year-end tax-planning and when.

Here's the thing. When the year's over, it's over for year-end tax planning. So you have to take action before 12/31 which means you need to plan before 12/31; early enough to have time to take action.

You need to determine now if you are going to push income or if you are going to pull it. Are you going to push or pull expenses. This is a huge factor. If you are going to push, you need to look at what you did last year because you might need to do the same thing this year.

The rule of thumb here is, reduce your income as much as you can, which can be achieved by pushing income into the upcoming year. I am not talking about putting cash and checks in the drawer, if you receive it; that's taxable. What I am talking about is delaying invoices to clients, or if you are a doctor, simply delaying when you turn in insurance claims. If you are doing those things then you could be in a situation where you collect the income next year. Follow?

To reduce your taxable income with prepaids, know this; you can pay up to 12 months of expenses in advance, and as long as you use that up within the 12 months, you can tax deduct that expense in the year paid.

Be smart when you get to year end. Focus in. I know you may be busy running your business and there are holidays to contend with but by doing this now, I promise it is going to save you taxes and you will be better prepared for the upcoming April.

Tax Strategies

How Many Toys Should I Buy? I Mean How Much Should I Spend on New Business Assets, For the Tax Deduction?

JJ THE CPA here. Let's talk about buying assets. Not toys. Business assets.

Copier, computer, machinery, vehicle, equipment, camera, etc. There are three different ways that you can get a full tax deduction for those. Get

Code Section 179.

Bonus depreciation.

Under $2,500 asset expense opportunity.

Let's start with this, when you get to yearend you should buy assets if you are looking to reduce your taxable income, but only if you think you are going to replace anything or need anything new between now and the end of next year. Why not just buy it now?

The first thing to ask yourself is can you afford it. You never want to spend money, just to save taxes. You need to do the assessment because if you can spend the money now and save the tax now, that might be a benefit as in essence it does reduce your overall cost of the asset; but only to the extent of the tax savings.

Let's say you buy $10,000 worth of assets, in computers, cameras, and printers. Now you are in a situation where that $10,000 could save you a third in taxes (an average percentage) or over $3,000.

Keep in mind that spending $10,000 is not going to save you $10,000, it's going to save you whatever your tax rate is. In this example, the $10,000 asset purchase that saved you $3,000 in taxes, is like it cost you $7,000. Follow? You still had to spend $10K.

Now let's talk about how you would actually buy that. We will discuss in the next chapter credit cards; but the key is, when you charge your credit card, that's when you get the tax deduction. It's not when you pay the credit card.

If you get a loan to buy something at year-end and it's a $50,000 piece of equipment that you need, and you are now going to finance that; if you are in a situation where you actually financed it and you signed at note, you get to write it off when you executed that note. Why? Signing the note is equal to buying it. If you were to buy it from a vendor at year-end and they tell you, you can just pay in January, that is not going to get you a tax deduction in the year you bought it, if you are cash basis, because you didn't pay for it. You just have a promise to pay and that does not necessarily mean that you get to write it off; that is just considered accounts payable.

When you are looking to buy assets make sure you can afford it, you need it, you are buying before year-end, whether with money, borrowing money or with your credit card.

Code section 179 has been around for a long time, under current tax law, up to one million dollars in business assets that you buy this year, you would be able to immediately deduct. The *catch* with Section 179, even though it's a beautiful provision in the tax law, is that you only get the deduction to the extent of your net taxable income. Example, you bought $100,000 worth of assets/equipment and your taxable income is $30,000. You'd only be able to deduct in the current year $30,000. The remaining $70,000 will carry over to next year. There are times that this makes sense and is a good strategy because if you can zero out your income in the current year and then take the rest of the deduction into the next year, that can save future taxes as well.

You might be in a situation where need the full deduction now, not caring if it yields a loss because you have other business interests that have net income, and you may like that loss to offset the other businesses net income.

So then you could take advantage of bonus depreciation, under current tax law. With bonus depreciation you are able to get a full deduction under the new tax law, which is a little ridiculous, but does not matter if it is new or used to get a 100% tax write-off, if you buy before year end. With no limitations on net income.

Third way is under a provision that came into play couple years ago. It is very complicated but to simplify it, if the asset is under $2,500 in cost to you, you can just expense it. What does that mean? It is not an asset that you are depreciating and it's not an asset that you are taking Section 179 or bonus depreciation against. The IRS basically allows you to just expense it like you would expense something like office supplies (paper, staples, etc.).

Regardless of what year you are reading this book, just like with anything, you need to consult with your CPA/EA on the actual allowable deductions you will realize in your specific situation. The tax law is always changing, and at any moment in time.

Tax Strategies

I Can Use My Credit Cards For Tax Planning? How?

JJ THE CPA here. Let's talk about credit cards and the year-end tax planning aspects of how to make sure that you are getting the deductions that you need and deserve.

There are some things that you really want to focus in on when you get to year-end and you are using your credit cards.

Again, the first thing to take note of is when you charge your credit card, that is when you get the deduction; it is not when you pay it off. The reason for that is that you now owe that credit card company, you no longer owe the vendor.

The other thing to note is when you pay off the credit card, that is not a tax deduction because you got the deduction when you charged the credit card. It will not help you to write a big check to the credit card company at year-end.

When you are using a credit card, especially days before year-end, you could be in a situation where the charge does not show up on your credit card statement until the following year. That is not a big deal, as long as you have the receipt to show the date you purchased the item, and the purchase was on or before 12/31.

The receipt is so key when it comes to this because that proves the deduction you are taking. Please, if you take anything away from this chapter, take away this, a credit card statement is near useless in proving an expense, if you are in audit. A credit card statement is not a receipt. The

IRS wants the actual receipt. Why? Because it proves the deduction and what the deduction is for. When you are looking at a credit card statement, it only shows the vendors name; it does not show what you purchased. You do still want to have your credit card statement, especially when you enter your information into your accounting software, QuickBooks. Just know it does not replace the receipt.

Make sure when you are entering your credit card statements into QuickBooks you are paying attention to the transactions that were done in December so you do not lose out on those possible deductions because not all credit card statements are from 12/1- 12/31. You may have a credit card statement that is from 12/10-1/11. So make sure you are paying attention to the dates of the transaction and that you are keeping all receipts to enter the charges in the correct tax year.

JJ THE CPA HERE!

In closing, I just wanted to say THANK YOU for buying and reading my book. It's my first, and I am honored you shared in my experience of becoming an author. I hope you found it useful, and brought some ideas forward to further discuss with your team of professionals. Be sure to check me out on social media, as I am sharing ideas every day, to extend the value of advice from a CPA.

I appreciate you!

www.ingramcontent.com/pod-product-compliance
Lightning Source LLC
Chambersburg PA
CBHW021349210526
45463CB00001B/38